An Altitude SuperGuide

Calgary Stampede

AND THE CANADIAN WEST

An Altitude SuperGuide

Calgary Stampede

AND THE CANADIAN WEST

by Patrick Tivy

Altitude Publishing Canada Ltd.
Canadian Rockies/Vancouver

Publication Information

Altitude Publishing Canada Ltd.
1500 Railway Avenue, PO Box 1410
Canmore, Alberta T0L 0M0

Copyright 1995 © Altitude
Text Copyright 1995 © Patrick Tivy

Canadian Cataloguing in Publication Data
Tivy, Patrick, 1945-
  The Calgary Exhibition and Stampede

(Altitude SuperGuide)
Includes index.
ISBN 1-55153-089-9
1. Calgary Stampede. 2. Rodeos--Alberta--Calgary.
I. Title. II. Series: SuperGuide.
GV1834.56.C22C3 1995 791.8'4'09712338
C95-910564-6

Made in Western Canada
Printed and bound in Canada
by Friesen Printers, Altona, Manitoba.

Altitude GreenTree Program
Altitude Publishing will plant in Western Canada twice as many trees as were used in the manufacturing of this product.

Front cover photo: Chuckwagons race at the
  Calgary Stampede
Frontispiece: The longest eight seconds
Back cover photo: Home on the ranch (top);
  the Calgary Stampede grounds, with the
  city skyline in the background (bottom)

Project Development
Concept/Art Direction	Stephen Hutchings
Design	Stephen Hutchings
Editing/Proofreading	Stephen Hutchings, Alison Barr
Index	Alison Barr
Electronic Page Layout	Stephen Hutchings
Financial Management	Laurie Smith

A Note from the Publisher
The world described in Altitude SuperGuides is a unique and fascinating place. It is a world filled with surprise and discovery, beauty and enjoyment, questions and answers. It is a world of people, cities, landscape, animals and wilderness as seen through the eyes of those who live in, work with, and care for this world. The process of describing this world is also a means of defining ourselves.

It is also a world of relationship, where people derive their meaning from a deep and abiding contact with the land – as well as from each other. And it is this sense of relationship that guides all of us at Altitude to ensure that these places continue to survive and evolve in the decades ahead.

Altitude SuperGuides are intended to be used as much as read. Like the world they describe, *Altitude SuperGuides* are evolving, adapting and growing. Please write to us with your comments and observations, and we will do our best to incorporate your ideas into future editions of these books.

Stephen Hutchings,
Publisher

Contents

The **Calgary Stampede SuperGuide** is organized according to the following colour scheme:

Information and introductory sections.........

Stampede sections ....

Historical sections...

Country Lifestyle sections ....

1. Introduction

The Alberta Rose, as hardy as the land, adapts to any conditions

The land of southern Alberta grows cowboys. It's a natural process, like wind and rain and the rising of the sun in the morning. Folks here have strong roots that run deep into the tough prairie soil. Elsewhere, tall trees turn some men into lumberjacks, and gold can make them into miners. Here, the great grasslands of Western Canada have created generations of men and women who spend their lives working with horses and cattle.

The image of the cowboy has been exploited all around the world, especially by the entertainment industries based in Hollywood and Nashville. Actors and singers have made millions of dollars simply by wearing cowboy hats. Advertising executives have launched national marketing campaigns on the cowboy theme, selling everything from cigarettes to political candidates.

The cowboy has been portrayed as the symbol of independence in countless movies, TV shows, radio dramas, novels, plays, and even poems. Because of all that, it's easy to think that cowboys and cowgirls are some kind of fictional inventions, like knights in shining armor and fair maidens locked in tall towers.

But in these parts, cowboyin' is just a fact of life.

It starts from the ground up. This area has been blessed with some of the finest pasture lands on the planet. Barely a century ago almost all of the West was one large grassy plain that stretched well beyond the horizon in all directions. There were open ranges the size of seas. Today the prairies have been carved up by railroads, fences and highways. Vast tracts are now occupied by grain farmers, or have been overtaken by cities, towns, and industrial developments. Even so, there are still plenty of ranches that are much larger than some of the smaller principalities of Europe.

The ranchlands were made for raising cattle. The prairie soils support a variety of grass types. Some are most nutritious in the spring, while others mature in the fall. For thousands of years before the coming of the pioneer settlers, the grasses fed buffalo by the millions. And after those huge herds were brought to the very brink of extinction, the early ranchers put cattle on the range. The cattle eat the same grasses and follow the same trails that the buffalo used to find water.

This is the land of the big sky. There are few trees, except in the sheltered river valleys or on the shaded hillsides along the foothills region near the Rocky Mountains. On the open prairie the whole world is divided evenly between land

The prairies reach to the Canadian Rocky Mountains in southern Alberta. This view is near Waterton Lakes National Park.

and sky, sliced neatly along the hard-edged line of the horizon. The heavens are an equal partner with the earth.

Together, soil and sky can determine the success or fail-

ure of the rancher's year. If moisture comes at the right time in the spring, there will be lush grass and maybe even a good hay crop. If not, if there is only a little snowfall during

winter, and if the spring rains fail, then it will be a hard year.

Vegetation is sparse over much of Western Canada's ranch country because the rainfall is scarce most years. All too often the big puffy rainclouds blow right by without letting a single drop fall to ground. The lack of moisture means that only the most hardy forms of grasses and shrubbery will survive. It also means that only the hardy ranchers can survive. The ones that fail are blown away like tumbleweeds. Cowboys are tough because they have to be. It is not an easy life.

Successful ranchers today have learned how to prosper by working with the ways of the land, not against them. They've adopted better methods of land management that do not expose the soil to the winds, and they take care not to overgraze.

Despite the rigors of the ranching life, the men and women involved in raising cattle have a deep emotional bond with the land they live and work on. They love few things more than the look of a greening field, or the sight of a calf or colt prancing on new grass. They live close to nature. They love the feel of the big sky all around them and feel hemmed in and trapped when they go to the big city for supplies. They know the melodic song of the meadowlark, the haunting shriek of the hawk, and the yipping chorus of the coyote.

The late evening sun casts a shadow of a solitary figure stretched out across the flat prairie grass

Cowboys will curse the vagaries of the cattle market, and fret constantly about the weather. They never have any real "time off" like city folks. In calving season, for instance, there simply is not any opportunity to take a holiday trip. The nearest neighbors may be many miles down a snow-choked road, but the distance means nothing because they are true friends who will do everything they can in a time of need. Folks in the country simply can't afford to behave as anonymous strangers .

Living close to the land creates a reverence for life, for basic truths, and for simple honesty. Standing alone under a clear blue sky and breathing in the clean Western air is good for the soul. It strengthens the love of freedom. That's what makes the cowboy way so appealing to men and women all around the world.

The First Nations

For thousands of years, the people of the First Nations lived in harmony with the land now called Western Canada. They were nomadic, and spent their lives following the buffalo, the sacred animal that provided them with food and the other essentials of life. Much of their story has been lost, but the basic strands have been traced and woven together by historians, archeologists, anthropologists and the great elders of the Native tribes who remember their people's oral history.

The people of the high plains in the West had a way of life all their own, entirely different from the groups who lived elsewhere. In forest regions, or near lakes and oceans, people would stay in one place much longer than on the grasslands. Then, as now, Westerners were people on the move.

Researchers are still not sure when the first people arrived on this continent. The earliest traces found in Alberta go back to the end of the last ice age around 11,000 years ago. Probably the people crossed over through a land

Buffalo

NO ONE CAN BE SURE how many buffalo there used to be. There were enough to cover the hills and valleys for three-day's ride in every direction. When a herd of buffalo was on the move, it could take most of a week for the great brown hairy river to pass a given point. There were that many, and more. Some experts calculate that there could have been as many as 60 million buffalo in the days before Columbus first crossed the Atlantic. Buffalo (also called bison) roamed over virtually the entire North American continent, from present-day Mexico to the Northwest Territories. They put a profound mark on the land.

The buffalo herds were in constant motion, always moving to fresh pastures. They ate the grass down to the ground and trampled everything they couldn't eat. Early explorers and hunters complained in their personal journals and official reports that after the buffalo had passed over a plain, there was nothing left for their horses. The herds ate the grasses they wanted and trampled all the bushes and small trees. In the spring, as they shed their thick winter coats, the buffalo would roll on their backs in the grass. They scoured the sod and left dusty "buffalo wallows" that could extend for several kilometres. They were four-legged, grass-fueled bulldozers.

The buffalo shaped the universe for the prairie Native tribes. According to many of the sacred stories of the prairie people, the buffalo was the Creator's finest gift to them. For thousands of years, the buffalo herds were their prime natural resource. The hunters would run the buffalo over cliffs, or trap them in corral-shaped pounds, and kill them with spears, arrows, and clubs.

Nothing was wasted. The animal's hairy coat was made into warm robes. The hide was made into teepee lodges, stretched tight and made into drums, sewn together to make bags and clothing. The bones, horns and hooves were made into tools and weapons.

By the early 1800's, the buffalo had been reduced to nearly 30 million as eastern Canada and the United States began to fill up with farms, towns, and cities. Then, shortly after the middle of the century, the slaughter of the buffalo grew more intense as railroads and "civilization" moved further West.

The massacre of the buffalo swept across the prairie with the intensity of a summer rainstorm. By 1870, it is estimated that there were only about 20 million left. Just 20 years later, the great herds disappeared. Only about 1,000 animals survived the holocaust. The bloody eradication of the buffalo destroyed the Native way of life and cleared the way for farmers and ranchers.

One of the first chores facing the pioneer settlers was picking up the buffalo bones that littered the plains. The bones were shipped east to factories where they were ground up and made into fertilizer. Once again, the buffalo was a prime resource. And again, nothing was wasted.

Buffalo

Remarkably, buffalo have made an astonishing comeback in recent decades. The revival of the buffalo is one of the grand success stories of the ecological conservation movement.

Scattered across Canada and the United States are hundreds of small herds of buffalo operated by private buffalo ranchers, by government agencies, or by Native tribes. The current population is estimated to be in excess of 200,000.

The Native tribes of Western Canada have taken a leadership role in the reintroduction of the buffalo. For them it represents a fundamental link to their cultural roots.

Raising buffalo is also a very profitable enterprise. Buffalo meat is low in fat and cholesterol and is very tasty, whether served as roasts, steaks, or ground and served as buffaloburgers.

Some buffalo ranchers also declare that, if handled properly, a buffalo herd is easier to deal with than cattle. Some say they have fewer problems with calving, and even maintain that buffalo are easier on the land because they don't turn a creek into a bog by gathering in one place as much as cattle do. They even say that buffalo can forage better on the land over winter.

The future is bright for the buffalo. Today, a full century after it came close to extinction, it still has a home on the Western range.

link that once connected Alaska and Siberia. Remarkably, even now the teepee used by the prairie tribes is almost identical with the yurt lodges of some nomadic Asians.

The tribes had no borders. The Tsuu T'Ina Nation (formerly called Sarcee), whose reserve is on Calgary's western city limits, came originally from northern Alberta and B.C., where they were part of the Beaver People. The group split off, migrated south, then split again. Now, branches of the group live in the Southwestern United States, where they are called the Apache and Navajo.

The Tsuu T'Ina were close allies with the Blackfoot Confederacy when the fur traders and explorers first came West. The Blackfoot, made up of the Siksika, the Blood, and the Peigan tribes, ruled most of the land that now makes up southern Alberta. The nearby Stoneys, who had originally come from the Ontario region, were on less-friendly terms.

Friend or foe, all the First Nations tribes in the area signed Treaty No. 7 in 1877, which put them under the protection of the British crown. Soon afterwards the world they knew ended. The buffalo disappeared and the Canadian Pacific Railway brought wave after wave of settlers.

Today, the members of the First Nations continue to honor to their cultural traditions as they participate more fully in the larger society.

2. The Ranch

Herding horses at the Calgary Stampede Ranch

I f rodeo horses dream, they probably dream of places like the Calgary Stampede Ranch. It's horse heaven, plain and simple. The Stampede Ranch has everything that a champion bucking horse could ever desire. It's laid out like a vast prairie playground in southern Alberta roughly

midway between Brooks and Hanna. The Stampede's horses have it all to themselves, except for the patch set aside for the rodeo bulls, and the fields where the Stampede's small herd of buffalo is kept. The Ranch is pure prairie, and most of it looks pretty much the same today as it did a thousand years ago, or even a thousand years before that.

Hardy dryland grasses, the kind cowboys call "prairie wool," cover the land like a bristly green blanket. Sturdy clumps of scrub willow are wrapped around the edges of the summer sloughs.

The Stampede herd is made up of about 325 horses, give or take a foal or two. The horses live on a virtual nature preserve. They share their wild kingdom with coyotes, rabbits, and rare burrowing owls. Hawks shriek as they circle

above, looking for gophers. Deer and pronghorn antelope still run free as the breeze, springing over the three-strand barbed wire fences as if they didn't exist.

The Ranch sprawls over slightly more than 34 sections. That's 34 old-fashioned square miles or roughly 55 square kilometres. Anywhere else, that would be considered a huge amount of land, but in the dryland parts of the ones are better for bareback events, and which ones can be trained for the saddle bronc event. Precise records of each horse's bloodline and bucking history are kept on computers.

Before they go the Stampede, the horses are given a few weeks of conditioning. They go for a long gallop three times a week to bring them up to the top level of fitness. When they're trucked long distances to remote events, like the National Finals Rodeo, they're given a couple of stops along the way to stay limber. They're hard working horses, but they certainly don't have to work for long. Each ride takes just eight seconds. They end up actually working only a few minutes each year.

The Stampede herd of bucking horses includes some of the top stars of the sport, broncs that have bucked at all the top rodeos in North America, from the Calgary Stampede to the National Finals Rodeo in the United States. For them, the Stampede Ranch is their nursery, their playground, their school, their lifelong family home, their hospital if they're ever ill, and at the end, their final resting place.

Cindy Rocket, for example, was one of the brightest stars to gallop over the ranch pastures. The pretty grey mare was foaled in 1960. By the age of three she was showing promise as a bucking horse. She went to the special exhibition rodeo at Expo '67 in Montreal and bucked in Vancouver

Relaxing at the ranch

prairies, it's in the middle rank. There are family ranches nearby that are more than twice the size of the Stampede Ranch.

The rodeo horses have that much space because they need it. The ranch is set in a part of the prairies that receives very little moisture from rain and snow. The Stampede herd is moved from one fenced-off field to another at regular intervals to prevent overgrazing. As much as possible, the horses are able to dine on fresh green grass, but if the rain fails to fall when it's needed, the Ranch cowboys bring in a few loads of hay.

The Ranch facilities include the old wooden corrals and chutes that were used previously at the Infield at Stampede Park in Calgary. There the horses are tested to see which ones will buck, which

The official Calgary Exhibition and Stampede brand

in 1969. She was an international champion, picking up both the Canadian Bareback title in 1970 at the Calgary Stampede, and the U.S. title at the National Finals Rodeo in 1969.

She was in constant demand at rodeos across the West because cowboys knew they were certain to get top marks if they were ever able to stay on top of her for the required eight seconds. She worked the rodeo circuit each summer from 1963 through to 1983 except when she was raising foals.

Cindy Rocket was formally honored at an official retirement ceremony at the Handhills Stampede on Wednesday, June 8, 1988. When she died in November the next year, her remains were laid to rest in the Broncos' Cemetery near the Ranch main gate. As a final honor, Cindy Rocket was inducted into the Canadian Rodeo Hall of Fame in 1993.

Today, her memory is kept perpetually alive by the dynasty of fine bucking horses she gave birth to over the years. Many of her foals have followed her hoofprints to the top rodeos in the land. And when they're not at work performing their eight-second chores at the rodeo, they frolic in the same grassy fields where Cindy Rocket galloped at the Stampede Ranch.

The cowboy horse

The pioneer West was built on the sturdy broad back of the cowboy horse. It was of no particular breed. Most often, the cowboy horse was a mix of several breeds, but it usually had a draft horse somewhere in its family tree. That gave the horse big healthy feet and solid bone structure to support muscles and tendons. The cowboy horse had strength and endurance so it could work all day and into the night.

Horses let loose at the Calgary Stampede Ranch

Today, the plain working horse has almost disappeared from the prairies and foothills. It's no longer needed for work, except on the largest ranches. And, sad to say, the old cowboy horse is not the first choice for competitional jumping or for recreational riding. The fashion today is for more elegant smaller-boned breeds, the Arabians, Quarter horses, and cross breeds with some Shetland pony in them. Now, for most folks, the only

Barbed Wire

BARBED WIRE IS NASTY, and beautiful, and practical, and even a bit poetic, all at the same time.

It's nasty when you get snagged on a barb. There isn't a cowboy alive who hasn't ripped his shirt or pants, or scratched his arm on the wicked stuff.

And it's beautiful because it's hardly there. It doesn't obscure the view the way a brick wall or a board fence would. Deer and antelope leap right over barbed wire, and coyotes and rabbits run under.

But it stops horses and cattle. It keeps them in the field where they belong, and that's why it's so darned practical.

As for the poetry, well, just listen to the wind whistling through a tightly-strung three-wire fence. The wires kind of hum and the barbs sort of rattle around. That's poetry, all right.

Old barbed wire has become a treasured collector's item and some wire fanciers are willing to pay more than $200 for a 45-centimetre length of a rare variety.

Cattle

THE ONLY REASON there are cowboys is because there are cows that need cowboys to look after them.

It's a tough job, even now when ranchers can take advantage of computers, automatic watering tanks, and artificial insemination. Today's cowboys have to deal with price fluctuations at the cattle market. They have to worry about ease of calving, weight-gain ratios, carcass yield, and trends in consumer marketing. It's a very complex and sophisticated business.

Beef cattle have been roaming over the Western Canadian landscape for much more than a century. They were here before barbed wire and in some areas were simply allowed to wander in search of feed. Cowboys rode herd on them, keeping them together and out of danger. The time of the open range was the classic era in the history of Canadian cowboying, when cowboys slept under the stars and sang around campfires. Later, the nature of the trade changed with the coming of smaller ranches enclosed by barbed wire. Ranchers began to specialize.

Today, cowboys are active in a great range of cattle enterprises, from supplying semen or fertilized embryos for registered breeding, to running a feedlot where young steers are fattened for market.

Cowboys have to take care of each animal, and devote great effort to its health. However, what's often more important is the health of the breed. If you ever want to hear a spirited debate, sit down between a pair of modern-minded stockgrowers who are discussing the merits of the Hereford in relation to the Belgian Blue, Brown Swiss, or Murray Grey.

A young contestant leads her prize cow to be judged

Cattle

They may not argue about which is the prettiest color, but they certainly will analyze in detail every other feature of each breed, from birth weight of calves, to carcass formation of butchered steers. They might agree that it's a matter of taste, and then declare that their favorite breed produces better steaks, roasts and hamburger patties. Two dairy farmers could match the war of words as they debate butterfat percentages, udder condition, and vitamin content.

The pioneer cattle breeds in the Canadian West came from Britain, the homeland of many of the biggest early ranchers. The black Angus, and the red and white Herefords and Shorthorns ate the grass that formerly had been food for the buffalo.

The British breeds flourished in the West. Even today they remain the foundation of the Western Canadian beef industry. Beef breeders have taken advantage of genetic research and can more easily identify traits that go into creating a successful and profitable herd.

Ranchers from around the world come to Western Canada to buy breeding stock to improve their herds. The Calgary Bull Sale held each spring at Stampede Park is one of the largest bull sales on the continent. Only Alberta-raised bulls are allowed. The beef breed shows at the Calgary Stampede in July include prize cattle from herds all across the country.

The introduction of the breeds from Europe and elsewhere has transformed the Canadian cattle industry in recent decades. The "exotics", such as Charolais and Limousin from France, Murray Grey from Australia, and Pinzgauer from Austria, have accelerated the popularity of hybrids which gain faster and produce a more efficient carcass. Cowboys have to care about such details. In their line of work, the profit margins really are close to the bone.

Despite the increasing sophistication of the cowboy business, there's still a little room for cowboy tomfoolery, as well as a wee bit of barnyard deception.

At cattle shows, for instance, it's not unusual to spend considerable time preparing an animal for the arena or sale ring. There's more to it than just giving a cow a shampoo.

The tail will be combed and fluffed up. Each hoof and horn will be cleaned and polished. The animal's coat will be thoroughly brushed, and sometimes powdered.

Some exhibitors get so caught up in the competition that they try to make up for the faults of nature. If a steer is underweight, for instance, they might give it a long drink of water using a garden hose.

And since they know that a good-looking animal will sell faster, they might cover up a patchy-looking hide with a generous coat of shoe polish or a light misting of spray paint.

One of the most daring tricks was pulled by a cowboy who had a steer with no tail. The animal had broken it off somehow. The cowboy went to the stockyards and got a tail from a butchered animal and tried to glue it on his steer. For a while, it looked as if his idea might work but the stunt backfired when the phoney tail fell off.

17

Papa Smurf *and* Go Wild *are two of the more famous Calgary Stampede bucking horses*

place left to see the old cowboy horse is at the rodeo.

The experts say that the first horses were about the size of dogs in prehistoric times and once rambled over the entire North American continent. Then they became extinct, but not before some of them migrated to China across the Siberia-Alaska land bridge. They didn't get back to their former pastures until Spanish soldiers arrived in Mexico with a herd of about 16 or 17 head in the year 1519.

Native hunters quickly became expert riders and traders. They spread the species northward. By 1730 the horse arrived in southern Alberta where it had a permanent impact on the way of life for the First Nations people. The horse made it easier to travel long distances, and to transport bulky loads. It became easier to hunt the buffalo, or make war on rival tribes. The First Nations people embraced the horse and adopted it into their mystic stories. Life is never the same after a horse enters your heart.

Horses were the most important means of travel for the early fur traders and explorers. The first great influx of horses from eastern Canada and the United States came as farms and ranches were established across the West. Horses were essential for pioneer agriculture. As the West became settled, stud farms in the foothills supplied stock to breeders around the world.

The supremacy of horses ended as cars and trucks rolled off the assembly lines. By the end of the Second World War, there were thousands of idle horses in the West that no one wanted or could afford to keep. They ran wild over farmlands that had been abandoned during the Depression, some still wearing shreds of the harness they had on when they were set free. But war-torn Europe was hungry, so a new market for horseflesh was

created, the canning industry. Even today, the can awaits horses that are old, infirm or that refuse to be ridden. They go to the can and then are warmly received in France or Japan.

Rodeo stock contractors

and chuck-wagon drivers buy up the horses no one else wants. They try to rescue as many horses as possible from the canners, but they're able to save only the good ones, the healthy horses that know how to buck, or can be trained to pull a wagon.

Strangely, not all horses can buck. Some kick and others make a dreadful noise, but they won't buck. And stranger still, there are many that are perfectly calm until the moment the rodeo chute gate opens. They relax nonchalantly as a cowboy

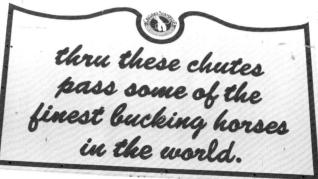

The Stampede ranch proudly displays this sign

puts on his saddle, and hardly blink as he climbs into the stirrups. Then they go to work bucking in true championship style, head down, hind legs kicking high for the sky. As soon as they get the cowboy off their back, they stop and trot for the exit gate. It's all a matter of their bloodlines and the training they receive.

One of the gentlest rodeo bucking horses of all time is Pawnee, a mild-mannered mare from the Stampede Ranch. She's as calm as a cream-fed kitten. She often visits shopping malls to meet people who've never

petted a bucking horse before. Pawnee is a real lady. She's so-phisticated. Some horses spook easily, but Pawnee doesn't mind taking rides up a freight elevator. She even allows little children to get up on her back. When a rodeo cowboy gets on top, however, Pawnee bucks.

Pawnee was two years old when she came to the Stampede Ranch and was registered as Stampede Horse No. 256.

"I've been trying to ride her for six months," Pawnee's previous owner told the Ranch cowboys. "I can't get her to stop bucking." Pawnee was on her way to the can for a few cents a pound when she was bought for the Ranch. Today, on the open market, "top end" rodeo horses are worth thousands. Pawnee has won the grass-for-life sweepstakes.

To help prompt the bucking instinct, a lightweight fleece-lined belt is strapped on bucking horses. The flankstrap causes no harm whatsoever but horses certainly try to buckit off, just like a kitten trying to shake off a piece of sticky

Wrangler

ED PUGH HAS BEEN cowboying "all my life, I guess." As a kid he rode to the Stampede in a chuckwagon, camping alongside the road at night. He has his own ranch but is also a Stampede Ranch cowboy:

"It was 50 years ago I first started working on the Stampede. I'm with the horses in the back there, behind the chutes.

"We cut horses in the morning for the event in the afternoon, I help do that. Then I flag the chute in the afternoon. I judged chuckwagons for 26 years, and I used to 'out-ride' there at one time, following the chuckwagons.

"As soon as they got the Stampede Ranch, we trailed the horses out there that summer from Calgary. It used to take us about four days. We had a Dude Wagon, took it along and slept in it. It was on four wheels and we pulled it with horses. Later years, we got pulling it with a truck. We called it the Dude Wagon.

"Horses are sort of like people, there's no two horses the same. They all act different. When you're trailing horses, you've got to slow 'em down. You got to stay right with 'em or they'll get away."

masking tape that accidentally got stuck on its paw. One of the pickup riders undoes the strap's quick-release buckle and removes it immediately after the cowboy is thrown, or is helped off the horse.

For almost 50 years, the bucking stock and other horses came to the Calgary Stampede on hoof, running through fields and along the grassy ditches beside country roads. But the practice stopped in the early 1960's as highways got busier and trucks for carrying horses got larger.

In 1987, the Stampede Ranch cowboys organized a revival of the old way. They rounded up the Stampede herd and trailed the horses all the way to Calgary.

"Trailing horses is becoming a lost art," says Stampede rodeo director Winston Bruce, who led the '87 operation. "A lot of guys try to drive horses, but you can't. You drive cattle, you get behind cattle and drive them along. But horses you trail, you get in front and they follow. They trail behind you. Sometimes you need to hold them back."

On the famous Trail of '87, the Stampede herd attracted great attention as it passed through small towns. Entire families gathered along the fence line to watch and wave to the cowboys as the historic procession rode by. Banquets were held each evening wherever the herd stopped for the night. It brought alive a million memories of the way things used to be.

"One of these years," says Bruce, "we're going to have to do that again."

Saddles

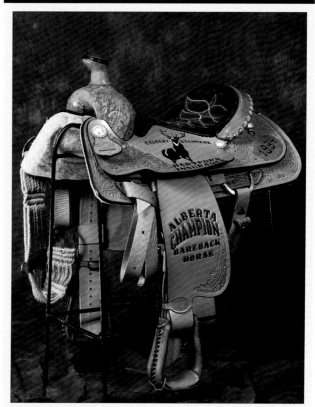

A COWBOY CAN grow to love his saddle. For cowboys, the saddle is a tool. It's his desk, his workbench, his operating console. A cowboy needs a good saddle to do his job.

That's because the saddle is the main contact point between a cowboy and his horse. A cowboy in a bad saddle is not a happy cowboy. A bad saddle is a pain in the butt.

The right saddle is a dream. It fits both horse and rider and rubs neither the wrong way. It's the correct type of saddle for the chores at hand. Western saddles are high in the back and front to help support the rider. A roper's saddle has a strong horn for attaching the lariat. Some are low-er in the back to allow the cowboy to swing his leg clear easily.

A good saddle will last a lifetime, and be passed on through the generations. Horses come, horses go, but the saddle stays the same. It's sometimes all a cowboy takes with him when he moves on. He could tell you the story behind every scar on the leather.

Some of the most precious saddles are rarely ridden. They are the prize saddles, great confections of tooled leather and shiny silver, won at a rodeo competition. Some cowboys have so many they put only the best on display in the house and leave the rest in the barn.

OLD RANCHES never seem to completely die. They merely fade away over a long period of time, preserving a sense of history through their continuing presence. These vestiges of our frontier past remind us of how life used to be, and to some extent, still is in the Canadian West. The abandoned barn (above) and the old horse-drawn cart (inset, right) are common sights in the western landscape.

3. Highlights of Stampede History

The Calgary Stampede Midway during the 1908 Dominion Exhibition

The Calgary Stampede wasn't called the Stampede when it began. It was called the Exhibition, or the Fair, and wasn't much different from all the other exhibitions and fairs across the land. It took a while for the Stampede to become a world-renowned, one-of-a-kind event. It was back in August of 1884 that a group of prominent Calgarians formed the Calgary and District Agricultural Society. They were too late to hold a fair that year, and they had to drop their plans for 1885 because of the North-West Rebellion.

They couldn't hold their first fair until October of 1886. It was a modest success, even though a blizzard kept many visitors and exhibitors away. In 1889, the society bought a large plot of land along the Elbow River. Today we call it Stampede Park.

The society members tried hard, but they couldn't keep the show going. A new group, the Inter-Western Pacific Exhibition Company, took over in 1899 and ran the fair until 1910, when the Calgary Industrial Exhibition Company was formed. With all those changes, it's clear that Calgarians weren't quite certain what they should do with their fair.

The man who had the an-swer was Guy Weadick. He cast one eye at the fairgrounds and saw a perfect place to put on a wild west show. Weadick had performed fancy rope tricks in Calgary in 1908 while touring with the famous 101 Ranch troupe. He was a born showman.

In 1912, with the help of the CPR's livestock agent, he rounded up four wealthy ranchers (known to this day as the Big Four) to provide finan-cial backing for a wild west show that would, he said, "make Buffalo Bill's Wild West Extravaganza look like a side show." The folks at the Exhibition went along and the first Stampede was held in September.

Weadick's first show was supposed to be a final farewell to the cowboy. It was nothing of the kind. As soon as the First World War was taken care of, he organized the Victory Stampede in 1919, which was even more successful than the first.

There were still many cautious Calgarians on the Exhibition board who weren't convinced, however. It wasn't until 1923 that the Exhibition and the Stampede were formally combined and became an annual event. Less than a decade later, the Stampede had become so popular that the name of the fair was legally changed. In 1932, the Indus-

Guy Weadick

trial Exhibition was renamed the Calgary Exhibition and Stampede Company.

That was also the year that Weadick's contract with the Stampede wasn't renewed.

The great Depression had hit Calgary hard and many members of the Stampede board resented Weadick's freewheeling attitude to money. He believed you had to spend money to make money. The old showman retired to his ranch near High River.

The rift wasn't healed until 1952, the 40th anniversary of his first Stampede, when he was the guest of honor and presented trophies to the winning cowboys. The reconciliation came just in time. In 1953, Weadick died.

Today, one of the most pleasant parts of Stampede Park is named in his honor. It's a little Western town called Weadickville.

It's a fitting tribute. It was Weadick who coaxed Calgarians to adopt the Western theme and make it their own. He encouraged local merchants to fancy up their shops at Stampede time, and asked ordinary citizens to dress in cowboy gear. It was Weadick who gave Calgary the Stampede.

And ever since, the Stampede has shown Calgarians and the rest of the world how to have a good time. The Stampede makes Calgary a special place to live in, and a thrilling place to visit. It's the Greatest Outdoor Show on Earth.

The Big Four

THE BIG FOUR WHO sponsored the 1912 Stampede were four wealthy ranchers—George Lane, Pat Burns, Archie McLean and A.E. Cross.

Burns and Cross were also two of the most prominent businessmen in Calgary. Burns ran a meatpacking company and Cross had a brewery. Lane and McLean had large ranches in the foothills.

They carried the first Stampede alone (each put up $25,000, a large amount then) and also helped finance the second Stampede in 1919. After that, the money end of things was left to the Exhibition board.

However, the Four continued to help out individually for many years. The Big Four Building is named in their honor.

A group of VIP's, including Charlie Russell and the Big Four, attend the 1919 Stampede

1847 A few rowdy cowboys make history when they take over a street in Santa Fe to show off their skills at roping cattle. A bemused visitor from the east writes a letter about the curious Western custom. It is the earliest known account of cowboy competition.

1872 Former Pony Express rider, stagecoach driver, buffalo hunter and U.S. Army scout William F. "Buffalo Bill" Cody opens a melodramatic show in Chicago portraying his Western adventures. In New York, the first of more than 1,700 dime novels is published about his exploits.

1875 North-West Mounted Police establish Fort Calgary to stop whiskey trade in foothills.

1877 Native tribes within two day's ride of Calgary sign Treaty 7, ensuring peaceful settlement of region.

1882 Cody expands his show for an "Old Glory Blow Out" on the Fourth of July in North Platte, Nebraska, with roughly 1,000 cowboys competing in the world's first rodeo show.

1883 Cody puts his wild west show on the road. He will perform in more than 1,000 cities and be seen by more than 60 million people around the world. His Wild West Extravaganza is one of the most popular shows of the era. CPR arrives at Calgary, village gets steel link with rest of world.

1884 Calgarians organize society to sponsor agricultural fair. Calgary (population: 506) becomes town.

1885 Guy Weadick born in Rochester, N.Y.

1886 Population of Calgary: 2,000. Attendance at town's first fair: 500.

1887 Cody show in London, presents special show for Queen Victoria and reaps publicity bonanza.

1889 Fair society buys land for fairground. They call it Victoria Park (later renamed Stampede Park).

1894 Calgary (pop.: 4,000) becomes city.

1905 Province of Alberta created.

1908 Weadick performs rope tricks at Dominion Exhibition in Calgary (pop.: 25,000).

1910 Horse population reaches peak. Decline sets in as new-fangled automobiles gain in popularity. Cody commences farewell tour.

1912 Weadick vows to make Cody's Extravaganza "look like a side show", presents first Calgary Stampede. Tom Three Persons wins Saddle Bronc Championship. Cody farewell tour continues.

1914 World war starts, hundreds of cowboys enlist. Cody farewell tour continues.

1915 Cody still on farewell tour.

1916 Calgary population: 56,514. Fair attendance: 103,433. Cody ends farewell tour.

1917 Buffalo Bill Cody,

winner of Medal of Honor and creator of spectacular Western entertainment, reaches end of life's trail.

1918 War ends.

1919 Weadick organizes Victory Stampede. Prince of Wales visits Calgary, falls in love with wild west, buys ranch in foothills.

1923 Calgary holds its third Stampede featuring world's first public chuckwagon races. The Stampede is formally made part of Exhibition, with Weadick on staff. Prince of Wales hosts rodeo champions at his ranch, and presents prizes. "Sorry, Prince," said bronc rider Pete Vandermeer when given engraved sterling silver cigarette case, "I don't smoke." He was given a gold watch instead.

1926 Dick Cosgrave sees his name engraved on Chuckwagon trophy for first time. It will be repeated nine times over the next 17 years

1931 Herman Linder starts six-year reign as Stampede All Around Cowboy. Clem Gardner wins Rangeland Derby.

1932 Hard times hit Stampede. Weadick is concerned with big decrease in prize money. Other disputes see him released from his contract. Board's corporate structure is reorganized and renamed Calgary Exhibition and Stampede Company. Johnny Left Hand wins Wild Cow Milking, a feat he will repeat in '44.

1937 Winston Bruce born at Stettler, grows up on rodeo ranch. He was later to become Rodeo Manager of the Calgary Exhibition and Stampede.

1939 Second World War starts in Europe.

1942 Stampede opened by four servicemen from army, navy, air force, and U.S. army.

1944 Calgary population: 97,241. Stampede attendance: 267,420.

1945 Second World War over. John Spotted Eagle wins Wild Horse Race.

1946 Patsy Rodgers was appointed to represent the city and Calgary Stampede at rodeos, in Madison Square Gardens in New York and in Boston, as Miss Rodeo Calgary. The first Stampede Queen contest was in 1947.

1948 Calgary's football team, the Stampeders, wins Grey Cup in Toronto. Fans go to game with Stampede gear and cowboy band.

1950 The Great Cosy Tibbs wins Stampede Saddle Bronc and Bareback titles.

1951 Special Stampede presented for Princess Elizabeth and husband Prince Philip in chilly October weather.

1952 Weadick returns as guest of honor at ceremonies celebrating 40th anniversary of first Stampede.

1953 Harry Dodging Horse wins Steer Decorating. Guy Weadick, founder of the Greatest Outdoor Show on Earth, reaches end of life's trail.

1954 Evelyn Eaglespeaker is Stampede Queen. Marty Wood wins first of five Stampede Saddle Bronc championships.

1955 Cliff Vandergrift wins fifth of eight Wild Horse Race titles at Stampede.

1959 Winston Bruce takes Stampede Saddle Bronc Championship and is also World Rookie of Year.

1961 Bruce is World Champion in Saddle Bronc.

1965 Walt Disney, creator of world's most famous theme parks, is honored as Parade Marshall. Disney, a long-time friend of Greatest Outdoor Show on Earth, also presides at opening ceremonies.

1966 Stampede opened by Robert F. Kennedy, candidate for U.S. presidency and brother of JFK. Flare Square honors oil industry.

1967 Stampede Week extended to nine days

1968 Stampede becomes a 10-day event

1970 Winston Bruce becomes Stampede Rodeo Director.

1973 Queen Elizabeth opens Stampede.

1974 New Grandstand built.

1976 Calgary population: 470,043. Stampede attendance: 1,015,682. First year Stampede breaks "magic million" mark.

1977 Charles, Prince of Wales, opens Stampede.

1979 First auction for chuckwagon canvas brings in top bid of $3,400.

1980 Flames hockey team moves from Atlanta to Calgary, putting city in National Hockey League.

1982 Start of Half Million Dollar Rodeo prizes.

1983 Saddledome built at Stampede Park.

1995 Dallas Dorchester gets record price of $125,000 at chuckwagon canvas auction.

4. Country Lifestyle

Now everyone can live Western. Not so long ago only those who had their homes in the hills were able to achieve a true Western lifestyle. That was the only place to find the various accoutrements that go into Western living. But fashions change, and now it is possible—even in

many of the largest cities—to locate the traditionally-styled furniture and furnishings that mark the Western way of life. For many people, the West is not a direction, it's a state of mind. They love the country way of life, and they are able to live it right in the heart of the urban jungle.

"Country style" once meant not having modern conveniences, especially plumbing. But today there's a new sense of sophistication to the country lifestyle. Now, country style means adding something extra.

It means decorating with authentic Western antiques, putting an old washstand to work as a cabinet for the TV set or the stereo, or making a new hand-crafted display shelf out of weathered old barn boards. It means hanging a horseshoe above the kitchen door, collecting prints by the late Charlie Russell, and

Cowboy clothing at work and at play: fashion follows function in country clothing

framing up old posters from the Calgary Stampede.

A Western-style house is a home of warmth, with warm colors and fabrics. Often that warmth will be made real with a fireplace or classic pot-belly

woodstove. The country kitchen will have a large wooden table, and pressed-back wooden chairs. The stove might be modern but there will be well-polished copper pots and black iron frying pans.

In the kitchen window might be an old coffee pot rescued from a derelict house now put to use as a planter. And in the flower-bed might be a battered wagon wheel covered with sweet peas.

There's something solid and honest about the Western lifestyle. It's based on the reality of hard work. From the very beginning in the days of the pioneer settlers, anything new that was made or bought for the home had to be built to last. There simply wasn't enough money to go round for stuff that would

The Calgary Stampede Look

DRESSING WESTERN is supposed to be fun. Of course, it is possible to take it all very seriously. Some of the rodeo cowboys at the Stampede certainly do, but they have good reasons for their perfectionist attitudes. They have a dress code to uphold. No one, after all, is allowed in the Stampede Infield without being properly dressed. That means they have to be wearing a cowboy hat as well as western-style pants and shirt.

The rodeo cowboys even compete for a special award, the Guy Weadick Trophy, which is presented to the cowboy who does the best job of presenting the true cowboy image in clothing, deportment, and sportsmanship.

Many ordinary Calgarians get totally involved, as well. They'll go to extremes with tailor-made Western suits, custom-made boots, and hand-crafted silver belt buckles and other accessories. They end up taking top prize at the fashion contests held at local nightspots.

Yet it is possible to "go Western" without going broke. Start with a pair of jeans, then get yourself a wide belt, and possibly a western shirt. Boots can be pricey and will last for years, so make sure they fit properly. At the very least, get yourself a cowboy hat. Even an inexpensive straw will do. Then wrap a bandanna around your neck and you're almost set.

There's just one thing left to do before you're really ready for the Calgary Stampede. Just lean your head back, open your mouth wide, and let loose with a Stampede yell: Yahoo!

Now you've got it!

Kettles boiling over an open cook fire epitomize life on the range

wear out in a season or two. Because of that, things that were part of the pioneer Western homestead were made of genuine leather, or brass and cast iron. Anything made of wood was built with solid wood, not tacky plastic veneers.

The pioneers had to keep their possessions in good repair, and quickly fixed anything that broke. They couldn't afford to throw it away and drive to the store to get another. Over the years, they filled their homes with much-loved objects that are regarded as priceless family heirlooms today.

Western themes can embellish every aspect of life. Today, men and women, even children, can dress Western from hat to boot. They can live in a Western-style home, and go to work or school in a pickup while listening to their country music singers. They can relax by reading Western novels, working on old-fashioned country crafts, or watch country music videos on TV.

Not everyone can work at an old-style Western occupation, but almost everyone can

The Calgary Stampede Connection

COWBOYS OWE A GREAT deal to the Calgary Stampede, and so does everyone else who loves the genuine Western lifestyle.

The Stampede is Canada's largest Western festival. The Calgary Exhibition and Stampede lasts just 10 days but it attracts close to one and a quarter million visitors each year. They come from all across Canada and around the world.

The Calgary Stampede is run by volunteers. It is dedicated to preserving and enhancing the agricultural and historical legacy of the West. It began life more than a century ago as an ambitious agricultural fair, a once-a-year gathering to provide a showcase for local produce.

Since then Stampede Park has grown into a year-round exhibition and sports facility. And the Stampede organization has become the nation's foremost exponent of the virtues of the Western way of life.

participate in Western sports like trail-riding or trick roping, and even some city slickers take part in rodeo events.

The country way of life was supposed to disappear ages ago. It was supposed to get paved out of existence by modern civilization. Yet like the old prairie grasses, it keeps coming back stronger than ever.

Country Clothing

You can ask a cowboy to ride up into the hills all alone at midnight through a springtime snowstorm to rescue a cow having trouble with a newborn calf.

You can count on a cowboy to get out in the mud in a howling rainstorm to help push a pickup truck out of a waterlogged bog-hole.

And you can even expect a cowboy not to grumble too much after being dragged through the barnyard muck by a mean-spirited steer.

Your average cowboy will perform the worst of chores and seldom will utter a discouraging word.

Just don't ask a cowboy to wear something uncomfortable.

So don't ever ask a cowboy to put on a necktie.

Save your breath. Don't even think of begging a cowboy not to wear jeans. If you want to invite a cowboy to a high-class formal occasion, he'll just reach into the back of his closet and haul out a crisp pair of black jeans that won't look out of place at the fanciest event. He may even slide into a western-styled jacket cut to look like a tuxedo coat. And if he absolutely needs to

Country fashion is suitable for the whole family...

wear a tie, he just might put on a bolo tie, or perhaps wrap a colorful silk bandanna around his neck.

These days, more than ever before, dressing western has

Bandanna

THE BANDANNA is the most dramatic element of essential cowboy gear.

In the old cowboy movies, the bad guys are always tugging their bandannas up to mask their faces as they get ready to rob the train. The good guys use their bandannas as temporary bandages when they get wounded in gunfights.

But despite the excesses of Hollywood movies, the bandanna is a very useful item. It keeps the neck warm in cool weather, and can be used to wipe away

sweat on hot days. Real cowboys still wear them. Cotton is the preferred fabric.

... no matter which way you face!

become high fashion. The growing popularity of country music stars and the surge of interest in country-style dancing has prompted a great wave of creativity in western wear for men and women of all ages. There's something for everyone in the whole family, from the tiniest of tiny tots to style-conscious comfort-loving seniors.

Western wear designers have broken loose from the old clichés. Jeans don't always have to be blue, for instance, and there's more than one style of boot available.

Manufacturers have become more attuned to the western wear marketplace and

Doug Lammle, Clothier

DOUG LAMMLE WORKED for many years at a major national retail store before setting up his own chain of western wear shops:

"Coming into this industry was like a godsend. The people are so much different. They live it. They breathe it from morning to night. Whether it's at work, whether it's at play, whatever, you're within the western wear industry. It's just absolutely phenomenal.

"There's a different attitude. It's a little more laid back on the surface, more hospitable, more genuine. There's an enormous amount of integrity amongst people, between suppliers and retailers, whereas in the other retail industry it's not that way; it's dot the I's, cross the T's, and look at your back.

"A lot of personal relationships are developed between retailers, between manufacturers, that make life interesting. Not to say the competition isn't fierce, but it isn't cut-throat, dog-eat-dog, stab-somebody-in-the-back. There's a lot more trust. I call it lifestyle, because you live it, and it's a lifestyle you want to live. It's comfortable."

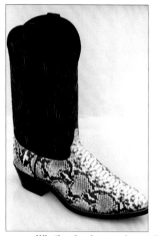

Whether for dress or for work (centre), cowboy boots are the first essential in any western outfit

Spurs

SPURS ARE THE ULTIMATE cowboy fashion accessory.

They separate the real horse-riding wrangler from the pretend variety, because nobody but a real cowboy knows how to walk properly with a pair of spurs strapped around his boots.

As for driving a pickup truck with spurs, forget it. Only an experienced driver can do that without getting all tangled up in the gas pedal.

Some horses seem to need the added emphasis of the spur to completely comprehend what a cowboy wants them to do. For many cowboys, spurs become an expression of their personality. Some want spurs that jingle and jangle, while others prefer the more sedate and silent kind.

Spurs are essential for rodeo competition, but the spurs must be dull so they won't injure the animal.

are using better fabrics. Gone are the days when most western wear garments were made from cheap polyester blends. The old take-it-or-leave-it philosophy is dead. Consumers today are demanding natural fabrics and retailers are meeting the demand with 100 per cent cotton shirts and blouses. The emphasis is on styling and comfortable fit.

And thanks to new social freedom at the workplace, casual-styled western wear is now welcome at the office, especially on so-called "blue jean Fridays". Western wear is gaining popularity as the first choice in year-round comfort clothing.

Many of the details of western styling can be traced to the traditional Spanish ranch clothing worn long ago in Mexico and the former Mexican territories, especially Texas and California. Today, the influence continues, especially in the "Santa Fe Look" from Arizona.

Great power comes from the decorative motifs created by the First Nations artists, designers and craftsmen. In more ways than one, the Western way of life is Native. Turquoise, the old sacred stone with mystical and magical powers, is framed with silver to decorate belt buckles and hat bands.

Western wear is practical clothing that emerged out of the down-to-the-earth workplace. It was originally made for hard-working men and women, and that spirit continues today as the designs are applied to durable and comfortable leisure wear.

Boots

A boot is just a boot unless it's a cowboy boot. Then it ceases to be mere footwear and becomes an expression of the wearer's personality. These days, a cowboy boot is often a symbol of good times, because more and more people are taking up western dancing, especially line dancing, and the only way to do that properly is in a pair of genuine cowboy boots.

Fortunately, boot manufacturers are tapping their toes to the same tune, and are now making boots to make dancing a pleasure, not a pain, by making boots with lower heels. They're also making boots shorter. The short boot is more flexible and stays cooler amid a round of hot dancing.

Heels in all heights. A short heel is called a walking heel. The tall type is a riding heel, because the high heel helps the boot lock into the stirrup while riding a horse. The riding heel is very popular with men and women who enjoy adding a few extra centimetres to their stature.

The most startling trend in bootwear is the roper boot, which features long lacing up the front. It's available in a vast variety of colors and styles for both women and men.

Pants, dresses and skirts

Cowboys, cowgirls, and ordinary folks who like the cowboy look—they come in all shapes and sizes. And now, finally, so do western pants, dresses and skirts. There was a time not so long ago when that was not the case. Then the only ones who could tuck themselves into cowboy jeans were people who had legs that were genuine cowboy legs, legs long and lean as a weathered fencepost. And most of the dresses were made of gingham and looked like checked tablecloths.

Now jeans come in a great variety of fits. There are still plenty of slim-line pants, but there are the more generous-cut styles as well. As well, jeans now come in a range of colors and fabric weights, so that it's possible to wear denim in the summer and not swelter in the sunshine.

Dresses have become more formal. There's less emphasis on the cute and more on the sophistication. Women's western wear has definitely grown up.

Some designers have even launched lines of western wear specifically intended for country-style weddings. The bride in the lacy white gown and matching lacy white hat stands beside the groom in the black jeans pants and tuxedo jacket with black felt hat.

Skirts and dresses for social occasions are often flared at the hem more than regular skirts. That's because the western style is designed for dancing, and that extra length looks its best when it's set whirling with all the swirling, spinning and fancy stepping.

Some dress and pant designers have made it easier to make coordinates by putting a small patch of patterned material on a skirt or pair of jeans that matches materials used in blouses and shirts. That little trick can certainly extend the versatility of a wardrobe.

Chaps

First of all, you have to know that

chaps are not chaps, they're shaps. It's a big difference, as vast as the gap between chips and ships. It's all in the pronunciation, of course. Chaps are jolly fellows from England, but shaps are sort of an extra pair of protective pants you strap on before saddling up and for a brisk ride through the buckbrush.

Chaps come in a great variety of types and styles, depending on the use and purpose. The kind made of woolly fleece help keep a cowboy's legs warm on cold fall and winter days. The fringe border on leather chaps helps keep the rain out of a cowboy's boots.

Rodeo athletes wear chaps to protect their legs from the occasional stray hoof or horn from a bucking bronc or bull. A well-aimed hoof will catch a grip on the fabric of a pair of jeans, but slippery leather chaps will deflect the blow. Chaps are the cowboy's answer to safety pads.

Belts and buckles

Western-style belts certainly do more than keep a pair of pants up. Belts and buckles can be veritable works of art. Most western pants have belt-loops made to take a 4-cm. (11/2-inch) wide belt. That's wide enough for a skilled leatherworker to create a unique fashion accessory. Some souvenir belts are inscribed with the wearer's name, or the name of the location they were purchased.

Buckles, however, are the most dramatic accessory of all.

A pair of chaps are left hanging on a wooden fence after a hard days work

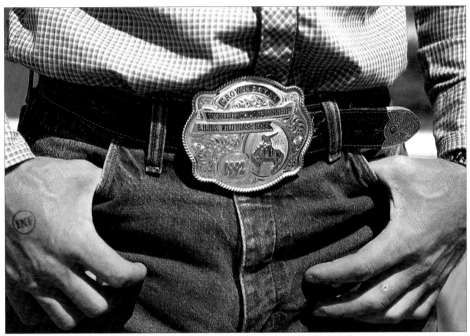

Buckles are worn for show—as well as for keeping the belt done up

The most gaudy buckles are prize buckles, the engraved buckles that are awarded to top rodeo athletes. They are silver billboards boasting of the wearer's accomplishments. When they're all polished up they shine like the headlights on new pickup truck.

Shirts and blouses

There are no rules, not when it comes to cowboy shirts. Anything goes. If you like it, wear it. Wear a shirt with a bandit collar, which is no collar at all.

As for colors, there's no end. And all possible patterns are acceptable. One half of a shirt might be blue, and the other half all black and red stripes. These shirts stand out.

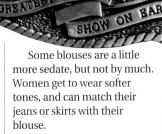

Some blouses are a little more sedate, but not by much. Women get to wear softer tones, and can match their jeans or skirts with their blouse.

One thing you'll hardly ever see on a rodeo athlete is a short-sleeved shirt, even on hot summer days. Long sleeves can help prevent scratches and bruises if the athlete has a hard landing in the infield.

Western fashion does have its fickle side. Even snap buttons, the most distinctive aspect of the western shirt, just about disappeared: Snap buttons used to be on each and every country-style shirt, from work-a-day polyester to fancy satin. The best had genuine mother-of-pearl

mounted in the metal snaps. The cheap ones had plastic, but they worked just as well. Snap buttons are easy to do up or undo—both ways, they're a snap. Best of all, they don't come off.

Snap buttons fell out of favor and were replaced with ordinary hole buttons on almost all shirts. It seemed the snap button tradition was gone for good. But nothing stays the same for long in the realm of fashion, not even for cowboys. In short order snap buttons began making a comeback as a nostalgia item. For cowboys who are short on sewing skills, that's mighty good news.

Hats

For men, there's no doubt about it. The top three colors for cowboy headgear are black, black, and black.

Black goes with just about anything. Black never shows dirt. And besides, Clint Black always wears a black hat.

Black hats made of felt are

Shape, style, colour and texture are all part of the selection when it comes time to make a decision: what type of cowboy hat is really "me"

the most expensive and the most stylish, but they're mighty hot in the summer. That's when it's time to switch to a straw hat. For variation, some favor an elegant grey felt.

White hats made of felt are special and usually are reserved for Stampede time. White straw matures and mellows as it ages, eventually acquiring a unique set of stains and scars that set it apart from all others. Old cowboys

know how to read a man's character in the way he wears his hat.

Whatever you do, don't refer to a cowboy's hat as a Stetson. At least, don't call it a Stetson unless it really is a genuine Stetson. The Stetson company makes excellent

hats, and does not want its name associated with other sorts.

For women's hats, the range of colors available is much larger, although women are less likely to wear a western hat. It all depends of the sort of statement that a woman wants to make with her western wardrobe. The color and styling of the hat must be chosen to complement her hairstyle and the rest of the ensemble.

Felt is never out of place and will never fall out of fashion, but the lighter straws are generally preferred for summer wear. And, as for men, white is the most popular color during Stampede.

Selecting a hatband is the finishing touch for a hat. Shiny silver is popular, and so is a simple leather strap. Fancier bands include elaborate feather creations, beadwork, or colorful Santa Fe designs.

Many rodeo athletes, both men and women, prefer to wear a felt hat while riding in competition, no matter how hot the weather. That's because a felt hat is considerably safer than a straw hat if an athlete takes a spill.

A felt hat can reduce bruising and possibly even prevent a concussion from a serious tumble. Straw hats create more risk of injury.

Besides, felt hats fly better than straw. Just watch a cowboy after he's completed a high-scoring ride on a bronc or bull. More often than not, he'll whip off his hat and throw it high into the air to celebrate. Straw hats are too flimsy for a victory toss. A champion rodeo cowboy will always insist on wearing a champion hat.

The White Hat

CALGARY JUST MIGHT be the only city on earth to adopt a hat as its symbol. The white hat has a long history. When the Governor-General visited in 1928, he and his wife were given white hats to wear to the Stampede.

And in 1946, flamboyant oilman Bill Herron and his family all wore white hats in the Stampede Parade. Then the hats received national recognition when a boisterous group of Calgarians wore them to the 1948 Grey Cup game in Toronto.

One of the leaders of the Grey Cup hi-jinks was radio announcer Don Mackay. When he became Mayor in 1949 Mackay began to offer hats as gifts to visiting celebrities. Since then the Calgary White Hat has become a symbol of Western hospitality.

Pickup Truck

COWBOYS DRIVE PICKUP trucks because pickup trucks are just about the only trucks that work as hard as cowboys do.

They are immensely practical vehicles. Pickup trucks can carry just about anything. You can haul hay in it all morning, then sweep it out and use it to bring home the groceries in the afternoon.

Pickups are high riders, so there's no problem getting the underframe hung up in a ditch when you're doing a little off-road rambling. And in town, that

Larry Shaw

LARRY SHAW has been selling pickups to cowboys and other truck enthusiasts for 25 years:

"What I'm always intrigued by is the different ways that people treat their pickups. We've seen chuckwagon drivers buy a pickup and two months later, the horse has kicked the door in, and they've run it down the side of the barn, and it looks like hell.

"And the next guy buys one and two years later it looks like he just drove it out of the showroom. He treats it like it's his baby. It's just the difference in the way people treat their possessions. For some it's just something to use and to beat the hell out of. But most of them are quite proud of their pickups."

means you can see clear over the cars ahead, so you can spot trouble down the road before you get to it.

Best of all, pickups have plenty of headroom for your hat when you get inside. Just sit back, turn the radio to the country station, and make yourself at home.

The West is the home of the pickup truck. Truck manufacturers sell more here than anywhere else. Cowboys drive them, oil-workers drive them, hard-working men and women of all kinds drive them. Country teenagers even use them for hotrodding.

A pickup is the closest thing to an old-fashioned buckboard or chuckwagon now available on four wheels. Until recently, the key feature of the pickup truck was the single bench seat. It was designed to accommodate a driver and one passenger comfortably and could handle a second passenger with ease.

However, it is possible to cram three, four, or even five riders up front along

with the driver. The big cowboys get in first and sit on the seat, then the short cowboys climb aboard and sit on the tall cowboys' laps.

In older pickups with floor-mount stickshifts, passengers stacked up in the middle have to keep their knees out of the way so the driver can grab for the gearshift knob.

Of course, being jammed that close together, they all have to be good friends. And if they aren't good friends when they start the trip, they certainly are at the end.

In warm weather, there's no reason for everyone to cram in front, not when there's room to ride outside in the back. If the box is empty, you can get the whole gang in there.

Truck manufacturers took some of the rustic charm out of pickups when they extended the cab and put in a rear seat. Some

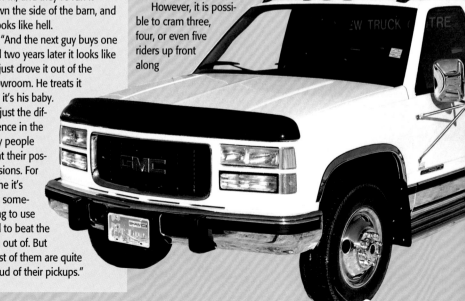

pickups come loaded with extras, like elegant upholstery, air conditioning, big stereos, box liners, four-wheel drive, chrome wheels, running lights and breezeway tailgates. No wonder pickups are sometimes called Cowboy Cadillacs. Fancy vans and minivans are taking a sizable slice of the traditional pickup market, but for the oldtime cowboy, nothing can ever replace the pickup.

The pickup truck is a solid part of the Western lifestyle and Western folklore. For instance, there's the old story about the two cowboys who met at the Calgary Stampede. One came from the Texas panhandle and the other was from the shortgrass country of Southern Alberta. They were bragging about the size of their ranches and about their pickups.

The Texan hooked his thumbs on his massive belt buckle, and said, "Let me tell you, my ranch is so big that I can get in my pickup at the first crack of dawn. I set out and I drive all morning, and I drive all afternoon. In fact, I can drive that pickup flat out all day long right clear until nightfall, and I'm still on my property."

The Alberta cowboy was silent for a moment. Finally he spoke. "Yep," he said, "I know what you mean. I had a pickup like that once, too."

Country music

Country music goes for the heart. Nothing else hits as hard as a country song. Country music has a dancing beat that makes the legs want to jump around. And the lyrics reach right out and caress the listener's ear.

Garth; Tanya; Tracy; Shania; Ian; Billy Ray; Cindy; Kostas; Sweethearts of the Rodeo; The Tractors; Dixie Chicks; Brooks; Dunn.

Country singers don't mess around. They sing about the real things of life. They turn on the emotional taps, from the warm fuzzy affection for pet dogs and old horses, to the sweaty passions of love, lust and remorse.

Well I'm shameless when it comes to lovin' you. All my ex's live in Texas. There was this woman and this man. Whose bed have your boots been under? There goes my heart breakin' in two. Nobody gets too much love.

Country music can't be stopped. Country songwriters create anthems that stir the soul. Country music is music you love. Country music loves you, and says so. Country stars seem somehow friendlier, more approachable, than other entertainment performers. We know them all on a first-name basis.

Randy; Dolly; Vince; Amy; Ricky; Kitty; Lorrie; Clint; Emmylou; Patricia; Alison; Wynonna; Merle; Trish; Porter; Nanci; Willie; Waylon; Reba; Clay; Pam.

Their voices are hot and sexy, warm and friendly, lonesome and mournful. They give an edge to each word so it can be heard over the sound of the engine of the pickup truck. There's a kind of tear in the voice that cuts like a knife, that slices into emotional bedrock, that opens the dusty wooden box where the deepest feelings are hidden.

C'mon baby, let's get out of this town. Baby, you can sleep while I drive. This time I know for sure. I never loved anyone like I love you. You can't make a heart love somebody. I love you 'cause I want to. I need you in my arms. I'm still lost on the lost highway. I believe in you.

Country music writers steal ideas from church music, newspaper headlines, foolish fads, folk tunes, jazz licks, rock and roll, and r&b. Singers can take tired old rock hits and give them new life with full country treatment.

Lari White; Patty Loveless; Collin Raye; Mark Collie; The Mavericks; Diamond Joe White; Anne Murray; Doug Stone; Faith Hill; Suzy Bogguss; Marty Stuart; Toby Keith. The Rankin Family; Prairie Oyster; Susan Aglukark.

There are no boundaries between styles of popular music. If a Country star does it, it's Country music. Country covers all fields like the green, green grass of home.

There's something women like about a pickup man. There's a truth in your eyes saying you'll never leave me. Stand by your man. Tell me I was dreaming, tell me that you didn't say goodbye.

Country singers are able explore the darkest sides of personal relationships, including adultery and divorce, alcohol and drugs, even poverty, prostitution and prison.

Mary Chapin Carpenter;

45

Jerry Jeff Walker; Michael Martin Murphy; Jimmy Dale Gilmore; Ricky Van Shelton; Joy Lynn White; John Michael Montgomery; Stacy Dean Campbell; Ricky Lynn Gregg; Lee Roy Parnell; Robert Earl Keen Jr; Hank Williams Jr; Junior Brown.

Country singers seem to live the songs they sing. Their problems with health and tax collectors make headlines. Their songs about domestic difficulties seem to come from personal experience.

You can dive to the bottom of your medicine jar, but wherever you go there you are. I'm old enough to know better but I'm still too young to care. Let's have a hometown honeymoon, just me and you.

Country music developed as a separate stream in the early days of the recording industry. Stars set a pattern for plain and simple styles that continue today, with sweet harmonies, steel-stringed guitars and classic Country fiddlin'.

Hank Williams; Patsy Cline; Vernon Dalhart; Hank Snow; The Carter Family; Spade Cooley; Gene Autry; Ferlin Husky;

Patricia Conroy performs frequently at the Stampede

Ernest Tubb; Johnny Cash; Milton Brown; Bill Monroe; Lester Flatt; Earl Scruggs. Wilf Carter; Bob Wills.

The video revolution has brought some singers and groups more exposure in a few minutes than many of the older performers got in a lifetime. Country singers have be-

Cindy Church, Country Music Singer

CINDY CHURCH PROVES that a Country voice can be at home in all styles of music. On her own, or accompanying other Country musicians, Cindy is as Country as they come. Her solo recording debut, *Love on the Range*, showed that her voice had the power to carry an entire album. She quickly followed it up with another, *Just a Little Rain*. Her success in the studio won her the title of Female Artist of the Year from the Alberta Country Music Association.

Cindy's voice has also added a pure, smooth Country texture to the vocal harmonies on the recordings she made with the Great Western Orchestra. Her distinctive voice can be heard doing backup behind such stars as Ian Tyson.

As a member of Quartette, the breath-taking Canadian supergroup made up of four powerful women singers, Cindy shows the full range of her versatility. The group's style includes cajun flavor, r & b, soul and gospel.

Cindy was born in Bible Hill in Nova Scotia, and now makes her home in Turner Valley, the ranching town set like a jewel in the Alberta foothills. With her partner, Nathan Tinkham, she continues to write and record.

Prairie Oyster, a popular Canadian Country music group, has appeared at the Calgary Stampede

come video idols across the land.

I'm somebody. Are you sure Hank done it this way? Your love amazes me. Half of my blood is Cain's blood, half of my blood is Abel's. You're so good when you're bad. Who do you know in California? I believe in you. Won't you take me with you.

Alabama; Kentucky Headhunters; Asleep at the Wheel; The Great Western Orchestra; Marshall Tucker Band; Little Texas; McBride & the Ride; Nitty Gritty Dirt Band; One Horse Blue; Pirates of the Mississippi; Boy Howdy; Evangeline.

The country music industry has formed strong alliances with video directors, television broadcasters and cable operators, and with major entertainment producers.

Nashville; The Opry; The Louisiana Hayride; South by Southwest at Austin; Dollyland; Pendleton; Cheyenne; Denver; The Calgary Stampede.

Ian Tyson, Country Music Singer

IAN TYSON WAS ALWAYS Country in his heart, but he spent many years on the folk circuit. You can take the singer out of the Country, but you can't take Country out of the singer. Country comes through.

Ian is one of Canada's national treasures. He's written, and sung, some of the best songs ever produced about the West.

There is simply no better song about the foothills area of Alberta than *Four Strong Winds*.

Someday Soon just might be the best song ever about rodeo.

Summer Wages says more about scufflin' around in Vancouver than three novels, two movies, and a CBC documentary. Ian's words paint perfect pictures. His tunes have hooks that never let go.

For a decade and more, Ian was half of a popular duet. But just like Simon and Garfunkel, Ian

and Sylvia eventually needed to go their separate ways. Ian's path led him to a ranch near Longview in the heart of Alberta cowboy country.

Slowly, the songwriter put down fresh roots and made himself at home in the Calgary music scene. He became a regular performer at the **Ranchman's**, Calgary's top Western club, and even married the innkeeper's daughter.

Food Fit for a Cowboy

NOBODY TODAY CAN match the genuine cowboy cooking style of a century ago. Nobody would dare.

If we can believe some of the historical reports, a cowboy's daily menu on the open range featured beans for breakfast, beans for lunch, and for supper, beans. As for a late-night snack, well, you could always have some more beans.

Beans are still an important part of cowboy cuisine, but fortunately the menu has grown considerably. Here are a few favorite recipes from the cowboy chefs at the Stampede's catering department.

BREAKFAST

During each Stampede it is estimated that at least 330,000 flapjacks are served at various Stampede breakfasts. Any pancake mix will do. The flapjacks are usually served with a few strips of bacon and a scoop of scrambled eggs. Some purists insist on rounding out the meal with, you guessed it, beans.

For a fancier breakfast, try this:

FLOUR TORTILLA WITH SCRAMBLED EGGS & JACK CHEESE

8 eggs scrambled.
5 oz. jack cheese grated.
4 green onions, finely chopped.
salt and pepper.
8 flour tortilla shells.

Combine scrambled eggs, grated cheese and green onion. Season with salt and pepper. Divide egg mixture among the 8 flour tortilla shells, roll up and seal one end. Bake at 325°F for 15 minutes. Serve with tomato salsa. Serves four.

LUNCH

Oh, go ahead. Be authentic and have beans.

CALGARY STAMPEDE BAKED BEANS

16 oz. baked beans.
4 oz. diced pineapple.
1/2 cup brown sugar
1/2 cup molasses
2 Tbsp. dry mustard
4 oz. bacon, diced
4 oz. onion, diced.

Sauté bacon and onion in pan. Combine all other ingredients in an ovenproof pot. Add bacon and onion mixture. Bake in oven at 350°F for 1/2 hour. Serves four.

Balance the beans with a fresh garden salad.

STAMPEDE DRESSING

Palomino dressing
6 oz. egg yolks.
14 oz. olive oil.
2 oz. lemon juice.
1 1/2 oz. red wine vinegar
1 1/2 rice wine
1 tsp. seasoning salt.
1/2 oz. dry mustard
1/2 tsp. oregano, crushed
salt and pepper
granulated onion
granulated garlic
Olive mixture
1 cup pitted whole green olives
4 oz. yellow onions (diced)
2 Tbsp. capers
dash of red pepper sauce
pinch of salt
1 oz. olive oil.

Place egg yolks in a bowl and blend with mixer about 1 minute. Slowly drizzle in oil, mixing constantly, until incorporated. Set aside. Combine remaining ingredients, except olive mixture. Mixing constantly, slowly add in the yolk-oil mixture. Then place olive mixture ingredients in food processor and blend until fine but not pasty. Using whip, blend olive mixture into yolk-oil mix. Transfer to a storage container, refrigerate until serving. Yield: 1 quart.

SUPPER

There's nothing better for supper than a fine cut of Alberta beef. Here's a way to add a little Stampede spice to a barbecue.

BARBECUED BEEF FLANK STEAK WITH CHARRED TOMATO SALSA

1/2 cup soy sauce
1/2 cup dry white wine
small onion chopped
3 Tbsp. Rosemary, chopped
2 Tbsp olive oil
2 garlic cloves, chopped
2 lb flank steak (serves six)

Combine all ingredients and marinate overnight. Drain steaks and barbecue. Serve with Charred Tomato Salsa.

CHARRED TOMATO SALSA

2 large tomatoes, pan roasted until blistered, black and soft
3 jalapeno chilies, charred until blistered and black
1 small white onion, thick sliced until golden brown
2 gloves garlic, pan roasted un til brown and soft, then peeled
1/4 tsp. dried oregano, toasted
1/4 tsp. cumin seed, toasted then ground
1/2 cup water
salt to taste

Chop tomatoes, chilies, onion. Combine ingredients for salsa.

Food Fit for a Cowboy

Serving up the always popular Stampede pancake breakfast

DESSERT

Here are two cowboy favorites.

RHUBARB CUSTARD PIE

(yield: one 9-inch pie)
  3 cups rhubarb cut into short pieces
  2 frozen 9-inch deep-dish pie shells, thawed
  1 cup sugar
  3 Tbsp. all purpose flour
  1 Tbsp. butter at room temperature
  1 Tsp. grated orange peel
  2 eggs, beaten to blend
  Preheat oven to 450°F. Arrange rhubarb in one pie shell. Blend sugar, flour, butter and orange peel in medium bowl. Add eggs and blend well. Pour over rhubarb. Take remaining pie shell and place on lightly-floured board, and roll dough flat. Cut dough into 1/2-inch strips, then arrange strips in lattice design on top of pie. Trim excess and pinch edge to seal. Bake 10 minutes at 450°F, then reduce to 350°F and continue baking until bubbly and golden (about 30 minutes). Serve at room temperature.

SLIM'S RUM CAKE

  500 g. vanilla cake base
  125 g. instant vanilla pudding
  4 whole eggs
  1/2 cup cold water
  1/2 cup vegetable oil
  1/3 chopped walnuts
  Mix together first five ingredients with mixer on low speed until smooth. Spray a bundt pan with vegetable oil spray and dust with flour. Sprinkle walnuts into bottom of pan and pour in the batter. Bake at 350°F for about one hour. Turn out the cake and poke full of holes. Pour the glaze over the cake.

GLAZE

  11/3 oz. butter melted
  1/2 oz. water
  11/3 oz. sugar
  4 oz. rum
  Add water and sugar to melted butter, mix well. Remove from heat and add rum.

LATE-NIGHT SNACKS

You could, of course, have beans again—baked beans, beans with pork, bean soup, or beans on toast. Or you could try something else:

STAMPEDE SAUSAGE SKEWERS

  1/4 cup chili sauce
  1/4 cup Holsin sauce
  3 Tbsp concentrated orange juice
  1 Tbsp grainy mustard
  1 Tbsp honey
  1/2 Tsp. crushed red chilies
  Fancy smoked sausages
  Cut sausages into thirds or slices. Stab sausages onto skewers (soak wooden skewers in water first) and barbecue over medium heat. Brush with basting sauce and turn often.

STAMPEDE VEGETABLE DIP

  1 cup mayonnaise
  1/2 Tbsp lemon juice
  1/4 Tsp salt
  1/4 paprika
  1/4 cup parsley, chopped
  1 Tbsp chives, chopped
  1/8 Tsp curry powder
  1/2 Tsp Worcestershire sauce
  1/2 cup sour cream
  Combine all ingredients and serve with a variety of favorite vegetables.

Guy Weadick (white shirt),
Mrs. Guy Weadick (Flors LeDue)
and Neil Hart (dark shirt)

Hollywood North

Hollywood stars shine brightly in Stampede country. Brad Pitt rode up into the foothills west of Calgary with Anthony Hopkins to film the classic ranch drama, *Legends of the Fall.*

During a break, Pitt came to Stampede Park to watch the Rangeland Derby. The racetrack was crowded but Pitt found a clear spot on the rail by the first turn. And there he was sprayed by chunks of dirt kicked up by the chuckwagon horses charging by.

Hollywood stars have a habit of getting up close to the action at the Stampede. Pitt is one the brightest new stars in Hollywood, but he's certainly not the first movie cowboy to rest his elbows on the rail at Stampede Park.

Tom Mix, one of the earliest and most famous cowboy actors, got hit by the same dirt. In fact, some Stampede oldtimers are certain that Pitt was standing exactly where Mix had stood, leaning on precisely the same section of the rail.

It could be true. The Hollywood connection is strong and goes back to the very beginning of the Stampede. Dozens of top stars who have their names engraved on the sidewalks along Hollywood Boulevard have come to Calgary so they could visit Stampede Park. They've charmed Stampede audiences, year after year.

It started with Guy Weadick even before he organized the first Stampede. Back in 1908, Weadick and Mix came

51

to Calgary with Hoot Gibson, trying to organize a wild west show. Later, Mix and Gibson both became big cowboy stars in Hollywood's silent movie days. They started the parade of stars from the Hollywood hills to Stampede country. Since then it's never stopped. Even Mickey and Minnie Mouse managed to get away from Disneyland to appear as Stampede parade marshalls in 1983.

Weadick and Gibson actually got to work together in 1925. Gibson brought his movie crew to Calgary to film a movie which became an international hit. The film was called *The Calgary Stampede*. Weadick was thrilled by the title. It provided fabulous free publicity for Calgary and helped boost attendance at the Stampede.

Weadick made a movie of his own three years later, filming *His Destiny*, a melodramatic cowboy drama. The movie was re-titled *North of 49* when it was released in the U.S. in order to emphasize its cowboy connections.

His Destiny was Weadick's last movie as well as his first,

The Ultimate Cowboy

THE ULTIMATE COWBOY is not an easy fella to pin down. *Ultimate* is the handsomest guy in the world, in a rugged sort of way. *Ultimate* doesn't say much, except when he's got something important to say. When *Ultimate* speaks, you just might want to listen up. *Ultimate* doesn't waste words.

You might not find the Ultimate Cowboy on every ranch, nor at every rodeo. The Ultimate Cowboy is the one we all carry in our hearts, the courageous cowboy who comes to life in books, movies, or videos.

He was Tom Mix in silent movie days. He was John Wayne in Technicolor. These days he can be Clint Eastwood or Clint Black.

No matter who portrays him, however, the Ultimate Cowboy is always on the side of truth and justice. He is often the last defence remaining against crime and evil.

His own tactics often might be less than innocent in the eyes of the law, but he is always of the side of good. His intentions are good, no matter what. He does

Although the Ultimate Cowboy is an imaginary figure found only in fiction, the desire to act out that legendary role is part of the dream shared by all cowboys throughout the Canadian west

Throughout his long history, the Ultimate Cowboy has always lived in the West. He is the man on the edge, who walks the fine line between the constraints of civilization and the freedom of nature. He has the power to work with nature, just as a ranch cowboy has the ability to train a wild horse to obey his command.

The Ultimate Cowboy rides through a landscape as stark and unforgiving as the situations he confronts. Invariably, there are few shades of grey. Evil is made plain. The bad guys are nasty to the core. They set fire to the wagons, blow up orphans and widows, and put poison in the wells. They cheat at cards and wear black hats. They fight dirty.

The odds are always overwhelming, but the Ultimate Cowboy fights with the strength of truth. He can knock out two scoundrels with one punch. He might get badly beaten, but he always manages to return in triumph. The good guy always wins in the end.

what's right, especially when no one else is able to. A man's gotta do what a man's gotta do.

The Ultimate Cowboy has left his mark on literature. He first gained popularity in the novels of James Fenimore Cooper. In Germany, he became Old Shatterhand in the books by Karl May. He's worn dozens of names in the novels of Louis L'Amour.

On television he was Hopalong Cassidy, Roy Rogers, Red Rider, and the Cisco Kid. In movies he's been Shane. He's even grabbed a guitar and become Gene Autry.

Brad Pitt and Aidan Quinn at the Calgary Stampede

but he maintained his Hollywood contacts. He got the most famous stars to visit, sometimes to perform at the Grandstand, or take part in official ceremonies, but often just to enjoy themselves.

The list of Hollywood stars at the Stampede over the years is like a Hall of Fame.

Douglas Fairbanks, Sr., was the most dashing movie hero of his day when he came to Calgary. Bob Hope was the most popular comedian when he made his appearance. Cary Grant was the most distinguished leading man.

Walt Disney was a living legend when he came to open the Stampede in 1965. Jack Oakie was one of Hollywood's finest actors in 1947 when he presided at the closing ceremonies. In 1959, Bing Crosby was just Bing Crosby, super-star singer, actor, and TV personality.

In the years when cowboy shows were the rage on TV, virtually all of the biggest stars joined the Stampede excitement, including Roy Rogers and Dale Evans, the Cisco Kid (Duncan Renaldo) and his sidekick Pancho (Leo Carillo), Jay Silverheels (Tonto in the *Lone Ranger* series), character actor Slim Pickens, Rex Allen (who played in *Frontier Doctor*), and Gene Barry (the dapper hero of the *Bat Masterson* series).

The goodwill created by the Stampede connection has helped the local movie industry. Veteran cowboys of the Calgary Stampede have appeared as stunt men in dozens of movies and television shows. Ranchers supply horses. Cowboys and recreational equestrians work as extras for movies that need a large number of riders.

Some of Hollywood's finest Western movies and Country music videos include scenes and sequences shot in Stampede country. There's such a variety of scenery, from barren desert canyons to blossoming mountain valleys.

Legends of the Fall was filmed in the same hills used two decades earlier for shooting *Little Big Man* with Dustin Hoffman. And not far away is the hillside near Longview where Clint Eastwood built himself a dusty pioneer town to film *The Unforgiven.*

Hollywood stars comes to Stampede country with make-believe stories. They anchor their movies and videos in the reality of the Western scenery.

Bat and the Plates

BAT MASTERSON WAS an unusual hero for a TV Western. He didn't wear dusty denims and wide-brimmed hat. Instead, he wore a dapper Western-styled suit and carried an elegant cane. Gene Barry played the part and made it his own.

Barry was a fine actor and had played a great range of roles, but he didn't realize how well he portrayed the legendary Masterson. When he came to the Stampede in 1959 he was surprised how many people called him Bat instead of Gene.

A phony shooting gallery was set up for part of Barry's performance at the Stampede. For safety's sake, trick plates were rigged to be broken on cue by hidden mousetraps.

Trouble was, one day the mousetraps went off too soon and broke the plates before Barry fired a single shot. It's hard to tell who got the biggest laugh, the audience or Barry himself.

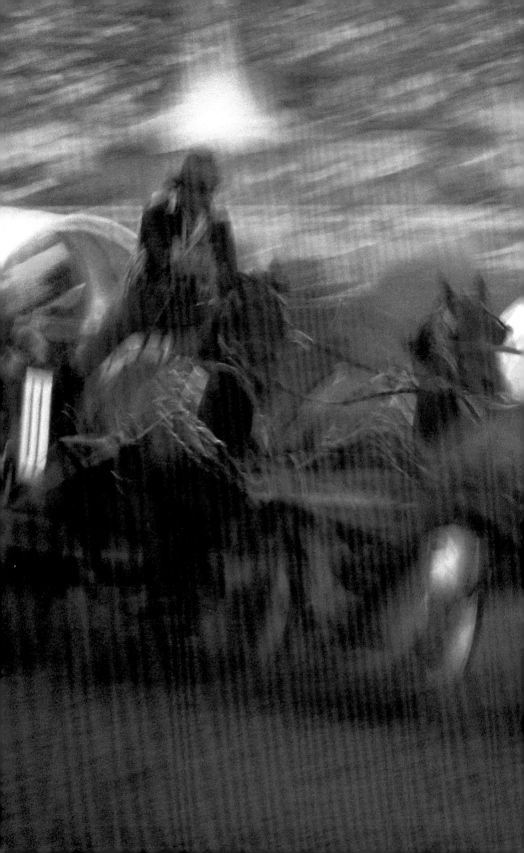

5. The Stampede Rodeo

Barrel racing, one of the most popular rodeo events, is fast and furious

Rodeo is the ultimate celebration of the wild side of the Western lifestyle. It's one of the fastest sports in the world. A good saddle bronc ride is over in just eight seconds and a bad one is over even sooner. For a rodeo cowboy, the Stampede rodeo competitions are the equivalent of the World Series or the World Cup. No other rodeo can match the cash offered as prize money at the Calgary Stampede.

Rodeo cowboys come from as far away as Texas, Australia, and Brazil to compete at Calgary. They all want to be the ones basking in the glory of Rodeo's Richest Hour.

At Rodeo's Richest Hour five cowboys are presented with trophies, belt buckles, championship rings, sponsorship bonuses, and Stampede Grand Prize cheques for $50,000 each. It's a moment that young cowboys dream about, and that old cowboys remember forever. Life just doesn't get any better.

Rodeo looks rough, tough and dangerous to some city folks, but it makes plain sense to anyone from the country. The events are competitive versions of ranch chores that once were routine. On any pioneer ranch, cowboys had to ride horses, haul wagons, and keep cattle from straying away. At the Stampede, these common cowboy skills are polished up, made safe for every man and beast, and presented as world-class sport.

The thrilling show has been at the very heart and soul of the Stampede from the very beginning in 1912. The major difference now is the array of rules and regulations which govern what happens at the Stampede. The Stampede judges can be very strict and will not tolerate anything that might injure an animal.

For instance, saddle bronc riders are given points for properly spurring the horse while holding onto a small halter with just one hand. The feet must stay in the stirrups and the free hand must not be used—cowboys are eliminated if they touch either the horse, the saddle or halter, or themselves with that free hand.

The athletes learn to work in a remarkable partnership with horses and cattle, the most powerful beasts of the ranch country. Rodeo horses and cattle are pampered like pet pussy cats. Many have a working day that's over in eight seconds or less.

One of the most exciting events of the Stampede is the Rangeland Derby. The Derby, a race featuring canvas-topped chuckwagons, is the Stampede's unique contribution to the world of sport. It started at Calgary and quickly spread across Western Canada. It hasn't caught on as much in the U.S. because many of the rodeo arenas don't have race tracks.

The rules are simple. The wagons take their positions in the Infield in front of the Grandstand. Then, when the signal sounds, they charge out onto the track. To give each outfit a fair start, they do a figure-8 loop around strategically-placed barrels.

Each wagon must have four outriders. At the start of the race the outriders must toss a mock stove and tent in the back—the "stoves" are made of rubber, because a real stove would be too dangerous

Chuckwagon Auction

WHAT IS THE VALUE of a champion cowboy? There is only one way to find out.

"He's for sale," declares the auctioneer.

"What am I bid? Who'll say ten thousand dollars?"

Standing squarely on the platform, staring the marketplace straight in the eye, is the chuckwagon driver, the hero of the Rangeland Derby.

In cowboy country, the chuckwagon driver pulls the most weight. He's a man of substance. He alone has the honor of putting himself in the same auction ring used to sell prize bulls.

Other cowboys earn their money one buck at a time. A fat wallet helps cushion the bruises. Chuckwagon drivers put their own cash on the line. A bronc rider can show up at the Stampede with just his saddle and the clothes on his back. A driver needs a wagon, a four-horse team, and a posse of outriders. It's a major investment.

To help pay the bills, the driver sells his wagon canvas as a billboard for advertisers. The purchasers include major oil companies, tire stores, dairies, meatpackers, banks and real es-

tate firms. To them, he sells his name and his race record. He sells himself.

As he steps up to the auction stage, the driver's record is read out loud. A tavern-sized video screen shows him in action racing at last year's Stampede.

For the middle-rank driver, the bidding starts low and climbs slow. For the top drivers the bids fly high right from the start. The auctioneer has trouble keeping them straight.

"Are you in or out? Forty-five thousand? Do I have fifty?"

When the canvas auction started in 1979, the top price was in the low four figures. Now a top driver can pick up more than one hundred thousand dollars.

All it takes is two bidders, both of whom have their hearts set on a particular driver, to start a bidding war. That way, the winning sponsors might end up paying much more for a driver than they planned.

Suddenly a cowboy discovers he's worth a lot more than anyone thought.

The auctioneer's hammer comes down.

"Sold!"

Winston Bruce, Rodeo Manager of the Calgary Stampede

WINSTON BRUCE, Rodeo Director of the Calgary Stampede, is a former world champion saddle bronc rider. He says the eight-second rodeo ride seems like forever:

"It's a big challenge riding an animal that doesn't want to be ridden, that has no set pattern. All it wants to do is win. It becomes a competition of skills, your's against his.

"There's a lot of mental imagery. In my case, because my father was a rodeo producer, he always had a lot of young, aspiring cowboys around. They taught me, so before I ever did it, I mentally had a good idea of what to do and when to do it.

"What you do is, you have the ability to have a video in your mind. You can turn that on and watch yourself riding different animals, and different styles of bucking performances, and see where your feet are, and your body position. You do that over and over, so that when you actually do get on the animal, it feels easy and natural. You go through a preparation of seeing yourself riding the animal many times over; perfect, always riding perfect.

"You arrive at a rodeo about a hour, an hour and a half, before the ride. You start gathering your equipment together. Your mind changes. It goes to heavy concentration to what you're going to do. Then as the animal is brought into the chute, you start preparing, putting your saddle and your tack on, then you become more concentrated. The outside world starts to shut off more all the time.

"By the time you get on the animal it's almost like being in a trance. You're totally alert, like really alert, but only alert to the things that matter at that moment, things like where the pickup men are, where the chute gate openers are, where the judges are, where the photographer may be.

"You get that fixed in your mind. Then you can feel the animal underneath you. He's usually quiet at that time because experienced horses are probably thinking the same things as you, only in reverse.

"By the time the chute gate is opened, the outside world is totally cut away. Your senses are really limited to only what matters at that moment in the arena.

"As you're riding the animal, you're aware of any movement around you, like the pickup horses or something flickering in the stands, because that could change the direction of the animal. You can usually sense a change of direction in the animal as it's happening.

"When the whistle blows, when the eight seconds are up, you know where the pickup men are. Then, when you get off the animal, your adrenaline is really running high and you feel good. And because of that, your alertness is on high, so there's a 'high' to that in the sense of satisfaction.

"It's always a personal contest against yourself, really. Everybody, I'm sure, has the same goal, and that goal is to make the perfect ride. That's what your goal is. You may never achieve it, but if you ever do, you're probably finished. Because what would you want to do the next time?"

Sometimes an eight second ride is just a dream

in case of accidents.

Today, there is a much higher level of professionalism in chuckwagon racing than before. Corporations pay thousands of dollars for the privilege of "renting" the advertising space on the canvas on the back of the wagon

The chuckwagon is the pioneer equivalent of the modern pickup truck. In the early days, whenever cowboys rode out to tend the herds, they would toss all their heavy gear into the chuckwagon. The wagon also carried the chuck, which is what cowboys sometimes call food. They often call it a lot worse names, but that depends on the cook.

Chuckwagon racing began in earnest at the 1923 Stampede. That was the first time in history that prizes were offered, but the idea goes back

much further than that. Racing is as old as time. The need to race is woven into human genetics.

It took Stampede founder Guy Weadick to turn it into an organized sport. The spark of

inspiration came in 1919 at the Victory Stampede, held to celebrate the end of the First World War. The scene was ready for excitement. All it needed was something to set it off. All it took was a couple of

Halters of some of the better-known Stampede horses

chuckwagons.

A few cowboys had parked two chuckwagons in front of the Grandstand and were cooking up some real rangeland grub for folks attending the Stampede. When the time came to pack up, one of the wagon drivers challenged the other to a race.

In a flash they both loaded their wagons, then rumbled down the racetrack to the exit. All the other cowboys jumped up on their horses and joined in. It was a great surprise. The Grandstand audience loved it.

Weadick knew a great idea when he saw one. He lined up enough chuckwagons for the next Stampede, held in 1923, to present a series of spectacular races to end the rodeo competitions each evening. It quickly became a one of the most popular Stampede events.

Rodeo is contagious. It gets in the blood and becomes a family tradition. The same family names rise to the top of the prize lists year after year, generation after generation. The best rodeo athletes usually come from rodeo families. Some rodeo cowboys will meet in competition and become friends for life. They get together after the day and socialize. They share expenses and take turns driving the pickup truck to the next rodeo.

Naturally, there's a broad streak of show biz in rodeo, but it's show biz with manure on its boots and honest sweat on the brow. Many of the athletes—from bullriders to barrel racers—are genuine farmers and ranchers when they aren't out on the rodeo circuit.

Large corporations have embraced the clean-cut cowboy image for their advertising and promotional purposes. Rodeo has developed strong links with the business community in recent years, following the pattern set by other professional sports. Companies of all types—from auto makers to breweries—are willing to launch major advertising campaigns based on cowboy themes and will pay many thousands of dollars for corporate sponsorships of rodeo events.

The commercial links, the media involvement, and the competition spurred by increased prize money have helped to raise rodeo standards and increase rodeo awareness all around the world. The athletes have formed professional associations and travel the circuits from one big show to another, often dropping in on small-town rodeos along the way.

Talent is always uppermost, but a large load of luck certainly helps in rodeo. In riding events, for instance, the rodeo judges base only half the score on a rider's ability; the other half is measured on how well the animal performs. A cowboy who draws a spirited animal will get higher marks if he can hang on. In Saddle

Bruce Flewelling, The Pickup Rider

BRUCE FLEWELLING HAS been riding pickup and helping contestants get off the bucking horses and bulls for more than 30 years. He also raises bucking horses for rodeos.

"I wasn't good enough to rodeo. But I wanted to be a part of it and there's no better place to watch your rodeos than from the pickup horse. I love doing it. One year I picked up 122 performances.

"The pickup man goes in there after the whistle blows and picks the cowboy up after his ride. You don't reach for him. They get off on you.

"You can't make a horse buck. It's bred in 'em, just like a race horse, or a cutting horse. You can't make 'em buck. There's some people think we're abusing them, making them buck. We don't. You can't. There's no way. If there was a way to make 'em buck, we would. A good bucking horse is worth a lot of money."

The wild horse race pits a team of cowboys against the horses and each other

Bronc and Bareback, the rider must keep his spurs touching the neck above the horse's shoulders. The spurs are made dull to prevent injury to the

A rodeo clown distracts a bull; many a cowboy owes his life to the timely intervention of the "clowns"

animal.

The roughest of the "roughstock" events is bull riding. In the Infield at all times is a rodeo clown with special skills. He is called a bullfighter, even though he doesn't actually fight the bull. The bullfighter's most important job in case a rider is tossed is to distract the bull so the rider can get clear without being trampled or gored.

Both calf roping and steer wrestling are based on the age-old chore of capturing cattle before they run away. In both events, the animal is let loose before the cowboy on horseback is allowed to start—going too soon results in a punishing 10-second penalty.

Calf roping is a test of horse and rider. The cowboy must lasso the calf, dismount, rely on his horse to stand still, run to the calf, deftly dump it on its side, and tie any three of its legs together. The cowboy gets back on his horse and allows the catch line to slacken. If the calf kicks free within six seconds, the cowboy is disqualified. Cowboys are also disqualified if the calf is jerked backwards head over heels during the lassoing.

There are separate sets of rules for each of the five big rodeo sports. Infringements mean additional penalty points that can put a contestant out of the money. There's even a dress code. Anyone who ventures into the Infield must be in western garb, especially wearing the wide-brimmed cowboy hat.

The Infield is a very special place and is treated with the same dignity and respect shown to championship golf courses, to tennis courts, and football fields. The eyes of the world are focused on the Infield during the Stampede. More than 16,000 spectators enjoy it from the comfortable seats of the Stampede Grandstand. A whopping seven million more viewers see it on television programs broadcast to every point on the planet. For rodeo cowboys around the world, the Stampede is the Big Time.

The Native Village is an active and popular attraction during the Stampede

First Nations at the Stampede

The First Nations people have been setting up their teepees in Stampede Park since the beginning of time.

At first the park was just another part of the valley lands along the banks of the Elbow river. It was a natural place to camp, if only for a night. There was always a good supply of water and firewood. There was good grazing land for horses. There was a good chance the hunters would find buffalo or deer.

Then, after the settlers came, the old hunting ground by the Elbow River became Calgary's fairgrounds, yet the Native people still camped there. They were invited to stay and participate in the races at the Exhibition, and later in the Stampede events.

Today, the pioneer town has become a huge city, but the teepee village continues to be one of the most popular attractions at the Stampede.

The Stampede is one of the most important organizations that has helped the tribes of the First Nations to preserve their Native heritage. From the days of the earliest fairs, and especially at the first Stampede, the Native people were invited to simply be themselves, to wear their Native clothing and present their remarkable dances. In the early days it was one of the few occasions when they weren't being asked to be imitation white

First Nations Pow Wow

THE DRUMMING AND singing at a First Nations Pow Wow is hauntingly powerful, and can have special significance for the Pow Wow musicians and dancers.

In most cases, the drummers and singers will not mind if visitors make private tape recordings of their songs. However, there are some songs that have spiritual meaning and that are to be treated with special respect. Generally, there will be an an-nouncement of the importance of such songs before the commencement of the dance. It would be regarded as quite improper and insulting to record a song of that type.

The same is true of some dance sequences.

In case of doubt, it is always better to ask permission before making a tape recording of a song, or taking a video of a dance.

A highlight of the Native activities is competitive Native dancing

tawa actually banned treaty Indians from going to the Stampede at all. Eventually, the Commissioner was convinced to revoke part of the ban. Elderly tribal members were allowed to go, but all able-bodied men and women were forbidden to attend. Fortunately the ban was never repeated.

For many years cowboys used to set up tents alongside the Indian Village at Stampede Park too. There weren't as many buildings then, so there was plenty of room for tents and wagons and teams of horses near the main entrance in the northwest corner of the park. The fragrant perfume of smoke from their campfires would drift over the noisy midway each evening, blending with the aromas of hot dogs, cotton candy and roasted corn. These days, some cowboys spend the night in motorhomes behind the chuckwagon stables. The teepee village has moved to a quiet poplar-sheltered area on the south side of Stampede Park.

Each day, several of the teepees are open for inspection. Inside, the owners often have on display a variety of historical artifacts. The beadwork is exceptionally fine. The designs painted on the teepee walls have deep meaning and often contain symbols of spiritual significance that were revealed to the teepee owner in dreams.

Native dancing displays are held every day during the Stampede but, in addition, the village hosts a three-day international Pow Wow featuring many of the finest competitive dancers on the continent.

people.

There were even some in the federal government who thought the Stampede should mind its own business, and not interfere with the official process of integrating the Native tribes into Canadian society. In 1925, the Commissioner of Indian Affairs in Ot-

The Stampede parade, which winds through the streets of downtown Calgary, signals the start of the Calgary Stampede

Stampede Events

When the Stampede is in full swing, you can see a blacksmith take a straight iron bar and turn it into a perfect horseshoe right before your eyes. Or you can stare in amazement at the machine that makes those tasty little doughnuts.

Then you can listen to a cowboy poet. Or dance your boots off to the music of a cowboy band.

You can even cheer on your favorite wee piggy in a pig race. Or try your luck at the Stampede Casino.

The action never stops. There's something going on, something to see, something to hear, something to do, in every corner of Stampede Park. The place is packed with magicians and musicians, hypnotists and jugglers, clowns and comedians.

Enter one building and see a tiny herd of miniature horses no taller than a table. Stroll through and see a prize-winning dairy cow. Then stop and admire an antique steam tractor.

It's all free once you're in Stampede Park. General gate admission costs about as much a movie, but the cost-conscious Stampeder can get free tickets or discount coupons from local retailers. There are free days for kids and for seniors. Tickets can be ordered in advance for the Grandstand Shows and for Saddledome concert performances.

Music

Think of it this way. The Stampede is Canada's largest and most exuberant music festival. At the Stampede, musicians play non-stop.

Brass bands march right through the milling crowds at Stampede Park. Rock legends of yesteryear and todays hottest stars play at open air stages in the shade of giant poplars. Young bands of astonishing talent perform in a temporary tent. Superstars shine in the Saddledome.

There's always a roster of fresh new entertainers, including some very hot young bands. There is something for every ear, for the patron who enjoys a good sing-along, and for the folks who want to boogie. The nightly Grandstand show always ends in spectacular fireworks.

The acts change rapidly through the week. There are even bandstands where you'd least expect them, like just around the corner from a guy trying to sell kitchen gadgets. That's the thing about the Stampede. There are always plenty of surprises.

The Royal Trio presides at Stampede events throughout the year (above left to right, from 1992, Princess, Kate McWhir; Queen, Shauna Oseen; Princess, Sherry Mitchell)

Each Stampede dozens of the finest floral arrangers in the Calgary region submit their best work for judging. Florists also demonstrate some of the inside tricks of artistic flower arranging.

Kitchen Theatre

Master chefs from some of Calgary's finest restaurants and catering services show how create culinary magic. Demonstrations are held approximately six times each day. Best of all, after each demonstration, members of the audience get to sample what the chefs have prepared.

Agricultural Showcase

The breeds of sheep, horses and cattle that have made western Canada famous for agricultural production are the centre of attention at the Stampede show rings. Stampede visitors are encouraged to tour the modern barns. You may even get to see a rancher using a hairdryer to fluff up the tail of a champion steer.

Cutting Horse Show

A good cutting horse does more than half the work when a cowboy is trying to pick a calf or steer out of a herd. The grace and intelligence of a cutting horse is displayed during this fascinating crowd-pleasing event.

Heavy Horse Show

There's hardly a sight on earth more thrilling than a matched team of heavy horses. Competitions are held in a variety of classes, including four-horse hitch, six-horse hitch, and a six-horse driving competition.

Western Art Gallery

Some of the finest Western-theme artists present an exhibition of their paintings and sculpture. The artists explore the traditions of the Western lifestyle. The themes and styles range from mythic interpretations to realistic depictions. Many artists tell stories in their art and strive for historical accuracy. The artworks are cast in bronze, painted on canvas, and etched on paper.

Handicrafts

Here is the greatest display of passion in Stampede Park. The articles on display are the result of countless hours of painstaking work. Not a stitch is out of place in the quilting, the knitting or sewing. Similar dedication to perfection is evident in woodworking, doll-making, painting, tole art, toys, and other crafts.

International Photo Salon

Proving again that the eye of the camera knows no borders, the International Photo Salon presents the best the world can offer. Each year roughly 400 photos are selected by the judges from more than 1,300 submissions. The photographers, both amateur and professional, present images captured on film in more than three dozen countries around the world.

Artisan Gallery

The finest arts and crafts are displayed by the artisans themselves. Demonstrations are presented at the individual booths and at the Creative Living Stage.

Floriad

Do as the old song says and take the time to smell the roses.

Volunteers

THERE'S ONE ACTIVITY that occurs at Stampede Park that hasn't got anywhere near half the recognition it deserves.

From the amount of time and energy that goes into it, there should be a trophy to honor the participants, or possibly an engraved belt buckle. At the very least, there should be a championship ribbon.

And what is this unsung, unrecognized, and unhonored event? It is the Stampede Volunteer Meeting.

Stampede volunteers seem to spend half their lives in Stampede meetings. The Stampede has roughly 1,650 volunteers. Each volunteer is assigned to one of 52 committees. Each committee has a specific task. There's one to supervise the Stampede Parade, another for the Downtown Attractions, and one each for all the various agricultural competitions.

Most of the committees meet once a month during the slow months, but the pace picks up as the Stampede events get closer. The monthly meetings become weekly, then daily. Many volunteers end up spending an entire week of their summer holidays at the Park during the Stampede. The Stampede simply couldn't exist without them.

The volunteers are the flesh and blood that bring the Stampede to life each year. They far outnumber the Stampede's 240 full-time employees and the 1,210 part-timers.

It's a tradition that began back when the Calgary and District Agricultural Society was first organized in 1884. The name of the group has changed, and its corporate structure is now much more complex, but it's still built on that same dedicated volunteer spirit.

The Stampede is a not-for-profit community-based company. There are roughly 900 shareholders who elect a board of directors. A volunteer has to survive

at least two years of Stampeding before they're asked if they'd like a voting share. Not everyone wants one. Volunteer burn-out reduces the ranks.

From the very beginning, many of the volunteers have been successful ranchers or high-powered executives of prominent companies. Calgary's Mayor is also a member of the board, along with two aldermen. The provincial government also has a representative.

Volunteers tend to stick to their areas of expertise. A member of the sheep committee, for instance, might never see anyone from the casino committee or the race promotion committee. The only time that everyone gets together is at the annual Showdown meeting held a few weeks before the Stampede starts. It's a bit of a pep rally at which the members pick up their Stampede badges.

The badges are another of the Stampede's traditions. They began as small identification pins that allowed the volunteers to have free admission at the Stampede Park gates. Over the years, however, they have become virtual works of ornamental art and are highly-prized by collectors.

One of the most important committees is the one that coordinates the Grandstand Show. For some reason it has attracted volunteers who just happen to be influential politicians. For many years the Grandstand commitee included former Alberta premier Peter Lougheed. Even now it's not unusual to see a cabinet minister pitching in to help plan the Grandstand's evening entertainment.

The Stampede lasts just 10 days but the volunteers are at it all year round. As soon as the dust has settled after one edition of the Greatest Show on Earth, the volunteers hold a meeting to discuss what went right, and what needs to be fixed for next year.

They repeat the process, year after year, Stampede after Stampede, meeting after meeting.

Opposite: *a future cowboy tries his hand with a lariat*

The Young Canadians are the basic ingredient of the nightly Stampede Grandstand Show

Stampede Programs

The Stampede is many things to many people.

For thousands of Calgarians and other residents of southern Alberta, Stampede Park is a year-round community activity centre.

Stampede Park is where hundreds of young children and teenagers learn to sing and dance, or to play a musical instrument. They take their first steps toward a career in entertainment, or develop a talent that will reward them with pleasure all their lives.

Kids from farms and ranches outside of Calgary come to Stampede Park for special events to learn the fine points of modern agriculture. And kids from the city come to get a close-up look at how farms and ranches operate.

Children with disabilities are always given a special treat at Stampede events. They'll have a Stampede Breakfast all their own, and meet some of the rodeo stars.

Young Canadians

The group with the highest profile is The Young Canadians. The troupe provides much of the entertainment each night during the Stampede Grandstand show, either by themselves or supporting a star headliner.

Today, more than 100 performers are in the troupe,

Randolph Avery

RANDOLPH AVERY is how the name was sometimes listed, but the man himself was always much more informal. To the thousands of young men and women who spent a term or two with the Young Canadians, however, he was just Randy.

Randy Avery was a showman and had been born to the trade. His mother worked on Broadway, "not as a star," he said, "but as a featured performer." He was on stage himself at the age of two.

During the Second World War, he presented shows for U.S. troops in Paris. Later, when he ran a major booking agency in Chicago, he was asked to put together the Grandstand Show for the Stampede.

He eventually moved to Calgary, organized The Young Canadians, and stayed active with the Stampede until his death in 1990. Today, his legacy lives on under the care of his son, Bill Avery.

A saxaphone player in the Stampede Show Band

the show must go on, is often put to the test during the Grandstand Show. It doesn't matter how rosy the weather report might be at the start of the Stampede, there's almost always a night or two when the rains come down. The young troupers always act like seasoned pros, even in a downpour, and keep the show moving briskly through to the end.

The Young Canadians of the Calgary Stampede were formally organized in 1968, but grew out of an earlier troupe, the Calgary Kidettes, that had been involved with the Grandstand show starting in 1964.

Stampede Band

More than 120 young musicians from across Calgary have toured the world as members of the Stampede Show Band. The smartly-dressed ambassadors provide music at all Stampede events and have spread the good word about the Stampede on their tours around the world.

4H on Parade

The farmers and ranchers of tomorrow get a look at the techniques they'll need to know be successful. As many as 600 to 700 teenagers participate in the weekend event, which features sessions with professional cattle judges and other experts.

Day on the Farm

In the spring each year, as many as 3,000 Calgary school children between the ages of 6 and 12 get a hands-on look at Alberta agriculture. The city kids learn how the food they eat arrived on the supermarket shelves.

Youth Talent Showdown

Talented young people from around southern Alberta compete at the Showdown during the Stampede. The Grand Award Winner gets $1,000, a trophy, and goes to Memphis, Tenn., for the North American finals.

Community Events

Virtually every day of the year somebody somewhere is benefiting from the Stampede's community outreach program. Depending on the needs of the particular event, the Stampede can provide a portable stage, some music or entertainment, or a visit by the Stampede Royalty, the Queen and Princesses. Other groups just want a Stampede poster or two, or some Grandstand tickets that they can raffle off for fundraising. During the Stampede, the Stampede Caravan takes the Stampede excitement to suburban shopping malls, where they get mall patrons into the swing of things with pancakes, musicians and rodeo stars.

including the junior singers and dancers, the apprentice groups, and the seniors. There is even a contingent of former members who return to the troupe for occasional appearances.

The Young Canadian School for the Performing Arts is where the performers learn the fine points of singing and dancing. With the gymnastics course, they learn the right way to do stunts on stage. Guest teachers from the world's entertainment capitals come to the school to conduct seminars. Like the school itself, the expert seminars are provided at no charge to the students.

The old theatrical adage,

Stampede Park

There's room enough at Stampede Park to display mammoth machinery used in the oil industry.

There are intimate spaces for small parties. There's room to exhibit a warehouse-load of fine art, antiques and collectibles.

Cattle, including prize bulls, are welcome at the Archie Boyce Theatre, which is very multi-functional. Visiting authors hold readings and book-signings at Rotary House, which is built like a charming old-fashioned log cabin.

Stampede Park is one of Calgary's busiest places, and one of the most adaptable. There's an appropriate space for just about any event, including ice shows, rock concerts, religious and service club gatherings, political rallies, banquets, business conferences, trade shows and conventions. Best of all, there's plenty of space for parking 2,500 vehicles of all sizes, including oversize off-road industrial machinery. All that and a casino.

Stampede Park hosts roughly 1100 events each year, on top of the grand 10-day Calgary Exhibition and Stampede festivities in July. The big show draws nearly 1.25 million visitors. During the 355 remaining days, the events at the Park bring in more than two million others.

There are nine rental spaces throughout the 137-acre Park, from the huge Roundup Centre, where the Stampede catering department can feed as many as 8,000 at one sitting, to small meeting rooms.

Many local businesses have turned to Stampede Park when searching for a handy venue for staff Christmas parties. There are even graduation parties, and the occasional wedding reception.

Special shows and sales that are open to the public are often held at Stampede Park, but many are restricted to invited guests from a particular industry.

Opposite: *The Stampede poster is an annual event, with each entry trying to set a new artistic standard*

6. Reference

The enduring life of the cowboy is one of western Canada's strongest characteristics

Resource Centres

You could fill a library with books about cowboyin' and the cowboy. In fact, at the **Glenbow Museum and Archives** in Calgary, they've done exactly that. The Glenbow is an essential resource for anyone wishing to conduct research into ranching history in Western Canada. The Glenbow's photo department will sell copies of historic cowboy photos and the lobby shop has a selection of authentic Native artifacts.

In the United States, similar exhibits and research facilities are open to the public. At Cody, Wyo., not far from Yellowstone National Park, is the **Buffalo Bill Historical Center**. It includes many personal and historical memorabilia related to the famous frontiersman and showman. There is also the **Cody Firearms Museum**, which is the largest and most important collection of U.S. firearms. The **Whitney Gallery** at the museum focuses on major Western artists from the 19th Century to the present day, including Remington, Russell, Schreyvogel and Moran.

The **Eiteljorg Museum** at Indianapolis, Ind., has a Western collection extending back to the early days of the 1800's and includes many fine examples of art from the Taos art colony in Taos, NM. The Native American collection features pottery, basketry, wood-carvings, and clothing from tribes across North America.

In Griffith Park, near the centre of Los Angeles, is the **Gene Autry Western Heritage Museum**, which has extensive displays of the real working West as well as exhibits showing how the cowboy's image has been depicted in novels, movies, television, and advertising.

At Tulsa, OK, the **Gilcrease Museum** has one of the largest collections of Native artifacts, as well as an extensive art collection and a large library dedicated to Western books.

Books

Writers have always been drawn like magnets to cowboys and the Old West. Some take a fictional approach, like

Louis L'Amour, while others restrict themselves to matters of fact. There are even writers who can't decide between fiction and fact and mix both, like the legendary Will James, who came from Quebec and fabricated a new life for himself in the United States. In any case, the result can be an entertaining read. Here are a few suggestions. Many, unfortunately, have gone out of print and have become rare collector's items. A diligent search might find a copy at a public library. Others are available in cheaper paperback editions.

Adams, Ramon. *Old-Time Cow Hand.* Toronto: Macmillan. 1961.

Baris, Ted, and Robert Semeniuk. *Rodeo Cowboys: The Last Heroes.* Edmonton: Executive Sport Publications. 1981.

Berton, Pierre. *Hollywood's Canada: The Americanization of our National Image.* Toronto: McClelland and Stewart. 1975.

Brado, Edward. *Cattle Kingdom: Early Ranching in Alberta.* Vancouver: Douglas and McIntyre. 1984.

Bruce, Jean. *The Last Best West.* Vancouver: Fitzhenry and Whiteside. 1976.

Cotton, E.J. Buffalo Bud: *Adventures of a Cowboy.* Vancouver: Hancock House. 1981.

Craig, John R. *Ranching with Lords and Commons.* Toronto: William Briggs. 1912.

Dary, David. *Cowboy Culture.* New York: Knopf. 1981.

Dempsey, Hugh A. *Calgary: Spirit of the West.* Saskatoon: Glenbow and Fifth House. 1994.

_____. *Indian Tribes of Alberta.* Calgary: Glenbow. 1988.

Evans, Simon M. Prince *Charming Goes West: The Story of the E.P. Ranch.* Calgary: University of Calgary Press. 1993.

Grant, Ted, and Andy Russell. *Men of the Saddle: Working Cowboys of Canada.* Toronto: Van Nostrand Reinhold. 1978.

Gray, James H. *A Brand of Its Own: The 100 Year History of the Calgary Exhibition and Stampede.* Saskatoon: Western Producer Prairie Books. 1985.

Kelly, L.V. *The Range Men.* Toronto: Coles Publishing. (reprint edition) 1970

Kramer, Pat. *Native Sites in Western Canada: An Altitude SuperGuide.* Banff/Canmore: Altitude. 1994.

MacEwan, Grant. *John Ware's Cow Country.* Saskatoon: Western Producer Prairie Books. 1976

Patterson, Bruce. *Alberta: An Altitude SuperGuide.* Banff: Altitude. 1992.

_____ and Mary McGuire. *The Wild West: An Altitude SuperGuide.* Banff: Altitude. 1993.

Rainbolt, Jo. *The Last Cowboy.* Helena: American & World Geographic Publishing. 1992.

Ward, Fay. *The Working Cowboy's Manual.* New York: Bonanza Press. 1983.

Whitney, Dudley. *Ranch.* Toronto: Key Porter. 1983.

Country Music

Of course, nothing matches a trip to Nashville, Tennessee. Check out Opryland, the Wildhorse Saloon, and the Ryman Auditorium where it all began.

Calgary has several nightspots dedicated to country music. Check local listings for current performers. For the latest hits, tune into a Country radio station, or watch the Country music video networks.

Movies

The movie channels are awash with excellent old movies, but here are a few that are worth making a special effort to see.

Unforgiven is one of the finest. It was made in the Alberta foothills in 1992 by Clint Eastwood.

Buffalo Bill and the Indians, or Sitting Bull's History Lesson, 1976. Director Robert Altman presents a revisionist version of Buffalo Bill, with Paul Newman in the starring role.

Little Big Man, 1970. Filmed on the Stoney reserve west of Calgary, this classic Hollywood epic starring Dustin Hoffman virtually created the Calgary film industry.

Western festivals

There's really only one. The Calgary Stampede.

Index

Index

Photo Credits

ALL PHOTOGRAPHS are courtesy The Calgary Exhibition and Stampede except for the following:
Patricia Conroy: 46
Stephen Hutchings: 31
Prairie Oyster: 47
Dennis Schmidt: 6, 7, 9, 10, 11, 22-3, 23 (inset), back cover (top)
Deidre Williams: 32 (bottom), 34 (middle top), 35, 37, 38, 39 (top), 52

Author Credits

THANKS TO Brian Brennan, Winston Bruce, Danny Copithorne, Hugh Dempsey, Bob Dinning, Sonya Dueck, Margaret Fraser, Brian Gamberg, Jim Hobart, Doug Lammle, Donnie Landis, Keith Marrington, Paul Mascioli, Maureen McCrimmon, Bob and Carol McKay, Robert Missen, Judy Pfeifer, Ed Pugh, Brian Ratcliffe, Genevieve Sawchyn, Larry Shaw, Dan Sullivan, Bill Tidball, and Grant Veno. And, again, to Valerie Boser.

The Author

THE AUTHOR Patrick Tivy was born in Calgary and is an alumnus of the University of Calgary. He has worked as copy editor, reporter, and columnist for both The Albertan and Calgary Herald newspapers, and as contributor to many magazines. For many years, he virtually lived at Stampede Park for a week in July while working as Crew Chief directing the Herald's Stampede coverage.

DATE DUE